LIVING THEORY
AS A WAY OF

LIVING THEORY RESEARCH AS A WAY OF LIFE

JACK WHITEHEAD

BROWN DOG BOOKS

First published 2018

Copyright © Jack Whitehead 2018

Published under licence by Brown Dog Books and
The Self-Publishing Partnership, 7 Green Park Station, Bath BA1 1JB

www.selfpublishingpartnership.co.uk

ISBN printed book: 978-1-78545-275-8

ISBN e-book: 978-1-78545-276-5

Design by Jenny Watson Design

Printed and bound by CPI Group (UK) Ltd, Croydon, CR0 4YY

ACKNOWLEDGEMENTS

I should like to thank all the Living Theory researchers I have worked and researched with during my professional life in education between 1967–2018. You have shared with me your life-affirming energy and the ontological and relational values you use in your living-theories to give meaning and purpose to your lives. You have also allowed me to share your living-theories on my web-site at http://www.actionresearch.net. I believe that our legacy is in our continuing contributions to Living Theory research as a social movement. This legacy is enhancing the flow of values and understandings that carry hope for the flourishing of humanity. Many thanks for the pleasure of your company.

Jack Whitehead, 17 March 2018

CONTENTS

INTRODUCTION

As you have worked on developing practice or knowledge as a contribution to a field or enterprise, have you ever thought, 'What's the point?' For fame or fortune? Or, given that you fulfil your contractual obligations to your employers, clients or customers, and make enough money to keep yourself and your nearest and dearest comfortable and in as good physical, emotional and mental health as possible, is there something in addition that is needed to understand why, what and how you do what you do and hold yourself to account to? A something that enables you to believe your life and work are not only satisfying and productive, but also worthwhile? Many psychologists have proposed various motivational theories, but while they are useful generalities, none of them enables me to explain what it is that gives my life and work meaning and purpose and whether I am making progress with respect to my standards of judgement. Those are questions that I have found Living Theory[1] research has enabled me to ask and evolve responses to that transform practice and knowledge in the process of researching them.

Everyone, irrespective of age, stage, context or field of practice, has an influence, for better or worse, in their own lives and learning and that of others. Some people, while trying to improve their field practice and contribute to knowledge of the world, also seek to improve their educational practice to have an educational influence in learning and life and contribute to educational knowledge. My understanding of what is 'educational' is learning that is concerned with both enhancing the realisation of one's own life-affirming and life-enhancing values in practice, and contributing to the flourishing of humanity, flourishing of my humanity, the humanity of other people, and the flourishing of humanity as a species.

I believe that each person has a responsibility to try to enhance their educational influence, while realising their other myriad responsibilities to: themselves; their family and friends; more distanced people such as employers and local community; and to contribute to the flourishing of humanity. This leads me to ask, 'how can I improve my practice (whatever that might be) and improve my educational influence in my own learning and life, the learning and lives of others, and the

---

1   In this book I have shortened Living Educational Theory research to Living Theory research. In the literature Living Theory research is sometimes written as 'living theory', which can be confused with an individual's living-theory. For clarity, in this book I distinguish between them by writing 'Living Theory' to indicate an approach to research and 'living-theory' to indicate an individual's explanation of their educational influences in learning. My understanding of what is educational is not restricted to what happens in 'education' organisations such as schools, colleges and universities. It embraces anyone's learning in life that includes values that carry hope for the flourishing of humanity.

social formations within which we live?' Such questions are often treated as though they are independent and have no relationship to the person asking them, even though scientists spend a lot of time trying to reduce the 'contamination' of the humans involved by, for instance, using randomised controlled trials. The attempt to take the researcher out of research that is developing practice and knowledge can be problematic in the physical sciences and even more so in the social sciences and educational research, which often try to emulate them; Living Theory research offers a productive resolution.

By engaging in Living Theory research, in the course of researching to improve field practice and knowledge, I clarify my relational and ontological values as they emerge and inform my efforts to improve my educational practice. I am also a knowledge-creator in the sense of creating knowledge in the form of explanations (theories) of my educational influences in learning. I shall be stressing the epistemological significance of recognising the unique constellation of an individual's values, as explanatory principles and living standards of judgement in my contribution to knowledge. I distinguish the individual's explanation of their educational influences in learning as their living-educational-theory[2]. The expression and clarification of the meanings of relational values draw on digital visual data that shows the Living Theory researcher existing in networks of continuously changing relationships within particular contexts.

I also draw insights from the theories of others to improve my practice and to deepen and extend my understandings of self and the sociohistorical and sociocultural influences in my practice and understandings.

My life-affirming and life-enhancing values enable me to explain and judge the success of my educational influence as I try to improve it. The values-based explanations of my educational influence in my own learning, the learning of others and the learning of social formations constitute my living-educational-theory, a term I coined in 1989 after two decades of research.

Between 1976 and 1989, I drew predominantly on the action-reflection cycles from an Action Research methodology. I continue to value the action-reflection cycles in my enquiry and I continue to address audiences of Action Researchers for instance in the Collaborative Action Research Network (CARN), the Action Research Network of the Americas (ARNA), the Action Learning Action Research Association (ALARA), the Bluewater Action Research Network (BARN), and the Network Educational Action Research Ireland (NEARI). As my enquiries increasingly focus on the generation of living-educational-theories and on

---

2   In the literature 'living-educational-theory' is sometimes abbreviated to 'living-theory'.

contributing to Living Theory as a social movement, I now stress the importance of using insights from other methodologies such as Self-Study, Autoethnography and Narrative Enquiry in the generation of a living-educational-theory and a living-theory methodology.

The eight (edited) papers in this book offer an introduction to Living Theory research and its implications for people who want to improve their educational influence and contribute to the growth of educational knowledge, as they work to improve practice and knowledge of a field, such as education, health, business, developmental economics, and community action. The papers emphasise the importance of clarifying, sharing and being accountable to the unique constellation of personal and relational ontological values we use to give meaning and purpose to our lives. The papers are organised chronologically from 1989 to 2018, each selected to clarify a particular point or aspect of Living Theory research, such as:

1. What constitutes a living-educational-theory.
2. Living Theory as a methodology.
3. Living logic.
4. The use of multimedia narrative to clarify and communicate the meanings of embodied values and their use as explanatory principles and living standards of judgement

Some have also been selected to clarify issues that have often arisen, such as:

1. The relationship between Living Theory research, other educational research and education research.
2. The relationship between Living Theory research and other forms of practitioner-research such as Self-Study, Action Research, Autoethnography and Narrative enquiry.
3. When a researcher has been told that they must select and apply a methodology at the beginning of their research, rather than trusting that their living theory methodology will emerge in the course of the enquiry and in the creation of a living-educational-theory.

Life and social contexts are in a process of continuous change. These papers show both my responses to these changes and my contributions to the changes. My purpose in producing this text is to share ideas that you may find useful in fulfilling your own life's purpose. My purpose is also to produce a record for myself that will move me into my next book with its focus on researching my contribution to Living Theory research as a social movement.

The eight papers in this book have offered an introduction to Living Theory research and its implications for people who want to understand, improve and explain their educational influence and contribute to the growth of educational knowledge, as they work to improve practice and knowledge of a field, such as education, health, business, developmental economics, and community action.

At the heart of the text is a sense of individual responsibility to live one's values and understandings as fully as possible in living a loving and productive life and in contributing to making the world a better place to be.

In Paper One, *Creating A Living-Educational-Theory From Questions Of The Kind, "How Do I Improve My Practice?"* I introduce the idea that each one of us could create and share their living-educational-theory as an explanation of educational influence in our own learning, the learning of others and the learning of social formations. I include this paper because it clarifies the nature of a living-educational-theory, living contradictions, values, validity, generalisability, and power relations. The implications of including 'I' as a living contradiction in an explanation raised the possibility that the logic of propositional theories, used in most academic texts, was mistaken. It was mistaken in its elimination of contradictions between statements in explanations of educational influences in learning.

Paper One also points to the use of embodied values as explanatory principles in explanations of educational influence. The meanings of embodied values are clarified and communicated in the course of their emergence in an educational enquiry. The importance of strengthening the validity of explanations includes the use of Popper's insight that objectivity is dependent on intersubjective criticism and that the validity could be strengthened with the help of validation groups that draw on Habermas' (1972, pp.2–3) criteria of social validity.

The idea of generalisability in traditional proposal theories, as explanations that apply to all, is replaced in Living Theory research by the idea of relatability in which the spreading influence of ideas from a living-educational-theory can be acknowledged in the generation and spreading of other living-educational-theories. The importance of understanding the power relations that influence the legitimation in higher education of educational knowledge, is also raised.

Paper Two, *How Do I Improve My Professional Practice As An Academic And Educational Manager? A Dialectical Analysis Of An Individual's Educational Development And A Basis For Socially Orientated Action Research*, is included because it clarifies a dialectical analysis, rational controls, validity and action-reflection cycles.

It demonstrates how a dialectical analysis can provide a valid explanation of an individual's educational influences in learning. The analysis included the use of action-reflection cycles to demonstrate the systematic nature of the educational enquiry. The importance of validity raised in Paper One is deepened and strengthened through the application of the mutual rational controls of critical discussion within validation groups.

Paper Three, *How Valid Are Multimedia Communications Of My Embodied Values In Living-Theories And Standards Of Educational Judgement And Practice?*, is included to explain the importance of digital visual data in a multimedia narrative. This includes the clarification and communication of the meanings of embodied expressions of energy-flowing values and their use as explanatory principles and living standards of judgement. It was only in 2004 that the University of Bath, in the UK, changed its regulations for the submission of research degrees to allow the submission of e-media, thus opening the way for the submission of multimedia narratives of explanations of educational influences in learning.

Paper Four, *Using A Living Theory Research Methodology In Improving Practice And Generating Educational Knowledge In Living Theories*, is included because it explicates meanings of an individual's living-theory methodology, living logic, education research, educational research, validity, values and digital visual data. The idea that each living-educational-theory involves the generation of a unique living-theory methodology in an educational enquiry of the form, 'How do I improve what I am doing?', challenges the view that an educational researcher must choose a methodological approach at the outset of the enquiry. A Living Theory researcher can draw insights from and use methods from different methodological approaches, without the emerging living-theory methodology being subsumed under any existing methodology. A clear distinction is drawn between education research and educational research, to make a similar point that a living-educational-theory cannot be subsumed within any existing theory from the disciplines of education. The previous Paper Three also highlighted the importance of digital visual data in clarifying and communicating the meanings of the expressions of embodied values, that are used as explanatory principles in explanations of educational influences in learning. Paper Four goes further than clarifying and communicating, in explicating a Living Theory research methodology.

Paper Five, *Generating Educational Theories That Can Explain Educational Influences In Learning,* is included because of its focus on knowledge-creators, units of appraisal, standards of judgement, living logics, energy-flowing values and empathetic resonance. I emphasise the importance, for the generation of educational knowledge, of Living Theory researchers seeing themselves as knowledge-creators. Understanding what it means to be a knowledge-creator involves the explication of the units of appraisal, standards of judgement and living logics that distinguish the nature of the contribution to educational knowledge. Explanatory principles in an explanation of educational influence are focused on energy-flowing values. The clarification and communication of the meanings of these values are focused on a method of empathetic resonance with digital visual data. This paper also demonstrates a critical and creative engagement with the literature and how ideas from the theories of others can be integrated within a living-educational-theory.

Paper Six, *A Living Logic For Educational Research*, is included because it further clarifies meanings of living logic, explanations of educational influences in the learning of others, reflection and reflexivity. Logic is described as a mode of thought that is appropriate for comprehending the real as rational. The living logic, in an explanation of educational influence in learning, requires both reflection and reflexivity.

Paper Seven, *Enacting Educational Reflexivity In Supervising Research Into Creating Living-Educational-Theories*, is included because it further clarifies meanings of educational reflexivity and a relationally dynamic awareness. These meanings include a relationally dynamic awareness in explicating the meanings of the relational and ontological values that an individual can use in explaining their educational influences in learning.

Paper Eight is composed of notes for doctoral and master's students, updated 28 January 2018, on *Justifying Your Creation Of A Living-Theory Methodology In The Creation Of Your Living-Educational-Theory*. This paper is included to stress the importance of resisting the application of a pre-existing methodology to your enquiry. It emphasises that a Living Theory researcher generates their own living-theory methodology in the creation of their living-educational-theory. The Living Theory researcher might, however, draw insights from existing methods and methodologies rather than choosing and then applying an existing methodology. The paper includes responses to Cresswell's ideas on: Narrative Research, Phenomenology, Grounded Theory, Ethnography and Case Studies; Ellis and Bochner's ideas on Auto-ethnography; Whitehead and McNiff's ideas on Action Research; Whitehead's ideas on Living Theory research; and Tight's ideas on Phenomenography.

PAPER ONE.

Whitehead, J. (1989) Creating a Living-Educational-Theory from Questions of the Kind, 'How Do I Improve My Practice?' *Cambridge Journal of Education*, 19(1); 41–52.

This paper is my most referenced paper. In relation to *Living Theory research as a way of life* it introduces readers to the idea of a living-educational-theory as an individual's explanation of their educational influences in their own learning, in the learning of others and in the learning of the social formations that influence practice and understanding. It grounds the generation of a living-educational-theory in asking, researching and answering questions of the kind, 'How do I improve my practice?', where the practice is an educational practice. The idea of a living-educational-theory is distinguished from the 'disciplines' approach to educational theory in which the theory is constituted by the conceptual frameworks and methods of validation of the disciplines of education.

A living-educational-theory involves learning with values that carry hope for the flourishing of humanity. The paper raises the issue of the 2,500-year history of the conflict between dialectical and formal logicians. The former claim that contradiction is the nucleus of dialectical theorising and central to social theories of change (Marcuse, 1964, p. 104). The latter claim that theories that contain contradictions are entirely useless as theory (Popper, 1963, p. 316).

The paper references the evidence from my enquiry, 'How do I improve my practice?', that grounds my Living Theory theorising in the exploration of the practical and theoretical implications of asking, researching and answering my question. I explain the importance of including the existence of 'I' as a living contradiction in my explanations of educational influence.

The theoretical implications include the clarification and communication of my ontological values in the course of their emergence in practice and their inclusion as explanatory principles in explanations of my educational influences. Their implications also include the integration of insights from propositional and dialectical theories in the generation of a living-educational-theory. The six sections of the paper focus on concerns that continue to interest me in **producing a living-educational-theory** as an explanation of educational influences in learning and in extending the influence of Living Theory research as a social movement.

1. 'How do I improve my practice?' – a question of methodology[3].
2. A question of acknowledging one's existence as a living contradiction.
3. How do we show our values in action?
4. How do we know that what the researcher says is true? – a question of validity.
5. How can we move from the individual to the universal? – a question of generalisability.
6. Which power relations influence the academic legitimacy of a living-educational-theory? – a question of the politics of truth.

This question of the politics of truth is highly relevant today with the media's communication of 'fake news' making it difficult to separate fact from fiction in establishing a valid explanation for what is happening in the world.

---

3   A living-educational-theory is not only concerned with improving practice. In the course of working and researching to improve practice an individual also generates and shares their explanation of educational influences in learning.

PAPER ONE.

Creating a Living-Educational-Theory from Questions of the Kind, 'How Do I Improve My Practice?'

Summary

This paper argues that a living-educational-theory of professional practice can be constructed from practitioners' enquiries of the kind, 'How do I improve my practice?' The significance of 'I' existing as a living contradiction in such enquiries is considered and other epistemological issues related to values, validity and generalisability are discussed from the living perspective. The process of gaining academic legitimation for a living form of theory is examined in terms of the politics of truth within our institutions of higher education.

Have you ever made a claim to know your own educational development and subjected the claim to public criticism? If you have, what does such a claim to educational knowledge look like?

I'm assuming that all readers of this journal will at some time have asked themselves questions of the kind, 'How do I improve my practice?' and will have endeavoured to improve some aspect of their practice. I believe that a systematic reflection on such a process provides insights into the nature of the descriptions and explanations, which we would accept as valid accounts of our educational development. I claim that a living-educational-theory will be produced from such accounts.

The idea that philosophers interpret the world whilst the point is to improve it is not a new idea. I have been urging my fellow academics for some years (Whitehead, 1982) to carry out an investigation into their own educational development as they question themselves on how they are improving their practice. I believe that academics who write about educational theory should do just that: make a claim to know their development and subject it to public criticism. In this way, I believe that they will come to see that it is possible to create a living-educational-theory that can be related directly to practice.

Producing A Living-Educational-Theory

The traditional view is that a theory is a general explanatory framework that can generate descriptions and explanations for empirically observed regularities and the behaviour of individual cases. The explanations are offered in the conceptual terms of propositions, which define determinate relationships between variables. Piagetian Cognitive Stage Theory is a classical example of such a theory. By their nature, concepts involve grasping principles, thus ensuring that theories are presented in general terms.

A commitment to the propositional form can also be seen, surprisingly, in those researchers who are committed to a reflexive approach to understanding. For example, Kilpatrick's (1951) view on the importance of dialogue in educational theory is presented in a propositional form. A more recent example, in the work of Gitlin and Goldstein (1987) on a dialogical approach to understanding, shows the authors presenting their case within a propositional form. Whilst I can recognise the importance of what they say about teachers forming relationships that enable school change to be based on a joint enquiry into what is really appropriate, I believe that the propositional form of presentation will prevent them getting closer to answering their final, dialogical question: 'How can we encourage the conditions necessary for teachers to enter into a dialogue aimed at understanding?'

Even those academics one would expect to understand the need to create an alternative to the propositional form of theory remain within it. For example, Donald Schön (1983) points out that:

> ... when someone reflects-in-action, he becomes a researcher in the practice context. He is not dependent on the categories of established theory and technique, but constructs a new theory of the unique case.

Schön is, however, committed to the fundamental category of established theory in holding to the propositional form:

> Theories are theories regardless of their origin: there are practical, common-sense theories as well as academic or scientific theories. A theory is not necessarily accepted, good, or true; it is only a set of interconnected propositions that have the same referent – the subject of the theory. Their interconnectedness is reflected in the logic of relationships among propositions: change in propositions at one point in the theory entails changes in propositions elsewhere in it.

> Theories are vehicles for explanation, prediction, explanatory theory explains events by setting forth propositions from which these events may be inferred, a predictive theory sets forth propositions from which inferences about future events may be made, and a theory of control describes the conditions under which events of a certain kind may be made to occur. In each case, the theory has an, 'if... then...' form (Argyris and Schön, 1975).

I am arguing that the propositional form is masking the living form and content of an educational theory that can generate valid descriptions and explanations for the educational development of individuals. This is not to deny the importance of propositional forms of understanding. I am arguing for a reconstruction of educational theory into a living form of question and answer, which includes propositional contributions from the traditional disciplines of education.

Gadamer (1975) points out that despite Plato we are still not ready for a logic of question and answer. He says that Collingwood (1978) helped to move us forward but died before he could develop this logic in a systematic way. Collingwood points out that if the meaning of a proposition is relative to the question it answers, its truth must be relative to the same thing. I agree with his point that meaning, agreement and contradiction, truth and falsehood, do not belong to propositions in their own right, they belong only to propositions as the answers to questions.

In saying that the theory should be in a living form, I recognise that this creates a fundamental problem. The way academics think about theory is constrained by propositional logic. All academics working in the field of educational theory present the theory in terms of propositional relationships. However, the purpose of my own text is to direct your attention to the living individuals and the contexts within which a living-theory is being produced (Lomax, 1986). Again, I wish to stress that this is not to deny the importance of propositional forms of understanding. In a living-educational-theory the logic of the propositional forms, whilst existing within the explanations given by practitioners in making sense of their practice, does not characterise the explanation. Rather the explanation is characterised by the logic of question and answer used in the exploration of questions of the form, 'How do I improve my practice?'

In developing such an approach I have had to come to terms with questions concerning an appropriate methodology for enquiries such as, 'How do I improve this process of education here?' In looking at videotapes of my practice I have had to confront the questions which arise on recognising the 'I' in the question as existing as a living contradiction. In the production of an explanation for my practice I have had to question how to include and present values whose meaning can only be clarified in the course of their emergence in practice. I have had to face questions related to validity and generalisability. I have also had to question the power relations, which influence the academic legitimacy of a living-educational-theory.

In such a short article all I can do is outline the present (1989) state of my thinking in relation to these questions.

'How Do I Improve My Practice?' – A Question Of Methodology

If we look at the locations where a living form of educational theory is being produced (Lomax, 1986; McNiff, 1988) we can trace the development of a number of teacher/researchers who have used the following form of action-reflection cycle for presenting their claims to know their own educational development as they investigate questions of the form, 'How do I improve this process of education here?':

- I experience problems when my educational values are negated in my practice.
- I imagine ways of overcoming my problems.
- I act on a chosen solution.
- I evaluate the outcomes of my actions.
- I modify my problems, ideas and actions in the light of my evaluations ... (and the cycle continues).
- This form of enquiry falls within the tradition of Action Research. It can be distinguished from other approaches in the tradition through its inclusion of 'I' as a living contradiction within the presentation of a claim to educational knowledge.

A Question Of Acknowledging One's Existence As A Living Contradiction

My insights about the nature of educational theory have been influenced by viewing videorecordings of my classroom practice. I could see that the 'I' in the question, 'How do I improve this process of education here?' existed as a living contradiction. By this I mean that 'I' contained two mutually exclusive opposites, the experience of holding educational values and the experience of their negation.

I searched the back issues of *Educational Theory* to see if I could find details of similar experiences reported by other researchers. I began to appreciate how the crucial issues of logic and values continued to reappear in the journal. From Cunningham's (1953) analysis of the *Extensional Limits of Aristotelian Logic*, through Mosier's (1967), *From Enquiry logic to Symbolic logic*, to Tostberg's (1976), *Observations of the Logic Bases of Educational Policy*, the debate about the logical basis of educational theory continues to rage in the literature.

A similar debate can be seen in the realm of values. We have, *The role of Value Theory in Education* (Butler, 1954), *Are Values Verifiable* (Bayles, 1960), *Education and some moves towards a Value Methodology* (Clayton, 1969) and *Knowledge and Values* (Smith, 1976). What these articles pick out is the continuing concern of educational researchers with the fundamental problems of logic and values in the production of educational theory.

I began to understand the concrete problems experienced by adherents to dialectical and propositional logics when they try to establish a sustained dialogue. The nucleus of dialectics, contradiction, is eliminated from descriptions and explanations presented in the propositional form (Popper, 1963). Dialecticians claim that the propositional form masks the dialectical nature of reality (Marcuse, 1964). I traced the tension between these logics to differences between Plato and Aristotle. In the Phaedrus, Socrates tells us that there are two ways of coming to know. We break things down into their separate components and we hold things together under a general idea. He says that those thinkers who can hold both the one and the many together he calls dialecticians. Aristotle, on the other hand, demands, in his work on interpretation, that the questioner puts his question into a definite form and asks whether or not a person has a particular characteristic or not. Aristotle's propositional logic eliminates contradictions from correct thought.

An understanding of a living form developed, in my case, from the combination of the following insight from Wittgenstein with visual records of practice:

> 'I' is not the name of a person, nor 'here' of a place, and 'this' is not a name. But they are connected with names. Names are explained by means of them. It is also true that it is characteristic of physics not to use these words. (Wittgenstein, 1953).

Now 'I', 'this' and 'here' are contained within questions of the form, 'How do I improve this process of education here?' In viewing videorecordings of our own educational practices I believe that we can see our own 'I's existing as living contradictions. This revelation, through the visual record, is crucial for the reconstruction of educational theory. Yet there is a tendency to reduce the significance of 'I' as it appears on a page of text. It is so easy to see the word 'I' and think of this as simply referring to a person. The 'I' remains formal and is rarely examined for content in itself. When you view yourself on video you can see and experience your 'I' containing content in itself. By this I mean that you see yourself as a living contradiction, holding educational values whilst at the same time negating them. Is it not such tension, caused by this contradiction, which moves us to imagine alternative ways of improving our situation? By integrating such contradictions in the presentations of our claims to know our educational practice we can construct descriptions and explanations for the educational development of individuals (King, 1987). Rather than conceive educational theory as a set of propositional relations from which we generate such descriptions and explanations, I am suggesting we produce educational theory in the living form of dialogues (Larter, 1987; Jensen, 1987), which have their focus in the descriptions and explanations which practitioners are producing for their own value-laden practice.

How Do We Show Our Values In Action?

The reason that values are fundamental to educational theory is that education is a value-laden practical activity. We cannot distinguish a process as education without making a value-judgement. I am taking such values to be the human goals which we use to give our lives their particular form. These values, which are embodied in our practice, are often referred to in terms such as freedom, justice, democracy (Peters, 1966), and love and productive work (Fromm, 1960). When offering an explanation for an individual's educational development these values can be used as reasons for action. For example, if a person is experiencing the negation of freedom, yet believes that she should be free, then the reason why she is acting to become free can be given in terms of freedom, i.e. I am acting in this way because I value my freedom. If someone asks why you are working to overcome anti-democratic forces in the workplace, then I believe that a commitment to the value of democracy would count as a reason to explain your actions. I do not believe that values are the types of qualities whose meanings can be communicated solely through a propositional form. I think values are embodied in our practice and their meaning can be communicated in the course of their emergence in practice. To understand the values, which move our educational development forward, I think we should start with records of our experience of their negation (Larter, 1985, 1987). I want to stress the importance of the visual records of our practice. In using such records we can both experience ourselves as living contradictions and communicate our understanding of the value-laden practical activity of education.

Through the use of videorecordings the teachers can engage in dialogues with colleagues about their practice. They can show the places where their values are negated. A clear understanding of these values can be shown to emerge in practice through time and struggle (Jensen, 1987). The kind of theory I have in mind forms part of the educational practices of the individuals concerned. It is not a theory, which can be constituted into a propositional form. It is a description and explanation of practice, which is part of the living form of the practice itself. I have suggested that a dialogical form enables such a theory to be presented for public criticism. Within this form the action-reflection cycle has been found (Lomax, 1986) to be an appropriate way of investigating questions of the kind, 'How do we improve this process of education here?' In this cycle we can study the gradual emergence of our values through time as we struggle to overcome the experience of their negation. We can describe and explain an individual's attempts to improve his or her educational practice (Foster, 1980). This approach to educational theory is being developed in a community of educational researchers who are committed to forming and sustaining a dialogical community (Bernstein, 1983) and who are willing to offer, for public criticism, records of their practice which are integrated within their claims to know this practice (Lomax, 1986). I am suggesting that a form of question and answer can also show how to incorporate insights in the conceptual terms of the traditional forms of knowledge whilst acknowledging the existence of ourselves as living contradictions as we refer to the records of our practice.

How Do We Know That What The Researcher Says Is True? – A Question Of Validity

Questions of validity are fundamentally important in all research, which is concerned with the generation and testing of theory. Researchers need to know what to use as the unit of appraisal and the standards of judgement in order to test a claim to educational knowledge. I suggest that the unit of appraisal is the individual's claim to know his or her educational development. Within this unit of appraisal, I use methodological, logical, ethical and aesthetic standards to judge the validity of the claim to knowledge (Whitehead and Foster, 1984).

Whilst most researchers may find it strange to take a unit of appraisal as their claim to know their educational development I think the unit is clearly comprehensible. My commitment to this unit owes a great deal to the work of Michael Polanyi. As I read *Personal Knowledge* (Polanyi, 1958), and reflected on my positivist approach to research (Whitehead, 1972), Polanyi's work fulfilled its purpose of 'stripping away the crippling mutilations which centuries of objectivist thought have imposed on the minds of men':

> In grounding my epistemology in *Personal Knowledge* I am conscious that I have taken a decision to understand the world from my own point of view, as a person claiming originality and exercising his personal judgement responsibly with universal intent. This commitment determines the nature of the unit of appraisal in my claim to knowledge. The unit is the individual's claim to know his or her own educational development (Whitehead, 1985).

I have given above some indication of the nature of the standards of judgement I use to test the validity of an individual's claim to know their own educational development. The questions I ask in judging the validity of the claim include:

a. Was the enquiry carried out in a systematic way? One methodological criterion I have used is the action-reflection cycle described above (Foster, 1980; Forrest, 1983).

b. Are the values used to distinguish the claim to knowledge as educational knowledge clearly shown and justified?

c. Does the claim contain evidence of a critical accommodation of propositional contributions from the traditional disciplines of education?

d. Are the assertions made in the claim clearly justified?

e. Is there evidence of an enquiring and critical approach to an educational problem?

I characterise the application of these criteria as an approach to social validation. They are related to Habermas' view on the claims to validity I am making if I wish to participate in a process of reaching an understanding with you. Habermas (1976) says that I must choose a comprehensible expression so that we can understand one another. I must have the intention of communicating a true proposition so that we can share my claim to knowledge. I must want to express my intentions truthfully so that we can believe what I say. Finally, I must choose an utterance that is right so that we can accept what I say and we can agree with one another with respect to a recognised normative background. Moreover, communicative action can continue undisturbed only as long as participants suppose that the validity claims they reciprocally raise are justified. However, such claims to knowledge may conform to acceptable standards of judgement yet still raise questions about their generalisability.

How Can We Move From The Individual To The Universal? – A Question Of Generalisability

Instead of thinking of an educational theory in terms of a set of propositional relationships between linguistic concepts, I am proposing a view of educational theory as a dynamic and living form whose content changes with the developing public conversations of those involved in its creation (Whitehead and Lomax, 1987). The theory is constituted by the practitioners' public descriptions and explanations of their own practice. The theory is located not solely within these accounts but in the relationship between the accounts and the practice. It is this relationship that constitutes the descriptions and explanations as a living form of theory. In being generated from the practices of individuals it has the capacity to relate directly to those practices. To the extent that the values underpinning the practices, the dialogues of question and answer and the systematic form of action-reflection cycle, are shared assumptions within this research community, then we are constructing an educational theory with some potential for generalisability. The 'general' in a living-theory still refers to 'all' but instead of being represented in a linguistic concept, 'all' refers to the shared form of life between the individuals constituting the theory. Now history shows us that new ideas have often met with scepticism, rejection or hostility from those who are working within the dominant paradigm. Researchers who are trying to make original and acknowledged contributions to their subject, education, might expect powerful opposition to their ideas.

Which Power Relations Influence The Academic Legitimacy Of A Living Educational Theory? – A Question Of The Politics Of Truth

My enquiry has led me to the question of how to support those power relations that support the autonomy of practical rationality within education. As part of this enquiry I think it important to examine the power relations that are distorting, undermining and systematically blocking the development of dialogical communities:

> ... In addition to the attempt to recover and reclaim the autonomy of practical rationality and show its relevance to all domains of culture, we realize that today the type of dialogical communities that are required for its flourishing are being distorted, undermined, and systematically blocked from coming into existence.... But today, when we seek for concrete exemplars of the types of dialogical communities in which practical rationality flourishes, we are at a much greater loss. Yet we can recognize how deeply rooted this frustrated aspiration is in human life (Bernstein, 1983).

Whilst this part of my enquiry is still embryonic I am continuing to study my own educational development as I engage with the following three problems.

A crucial issue in gaining academic legitimacy for a particular view of educational theory concerns the institutional arrangements for appointing examiners for research degrees in Education. For example, in some institutions a student is not permitted, under any circumstances, to question the competence of an examiner once the examiner has been appointed by the Senate. Given that the academics in one such institution have committed themselves to the statement, 'A University has a moral purpose in society in the sense of upholding certain standards of truth, freedom and democracy', this raises a question on how the academics are upholding these values.

I wish to question the power relations which sustain the view that competence is a matter of appointment, rather than of judgement, on the grounds that any academic judgement should, as a matter of principle, be open to criticism and to the possibility of incompetence. Could any academic keep his or her integrity and at the same time accept the truth of power which sustains the view that no questions of competence can be raised in the light of actual judgements?

I argue that, on principle, the power of truth is served by permitting such a challenge in relation to an examiner's judgement, rather than seeing competence to be a procedural matter of appointment.

The second problem concerns the problem of self-identification in texts for publication. A problem I would have had in sending this work to a refereed journal such as *Educational Theory*. The problem follows from a central point in this paper that academics and practitioners should identify themselves in their work context and, at some point in their research, offer for public criticism a claim to know their own educational development. However, the guidelines and procedures of the staff of *Educational Theory* state:

> Manuscripts are subjected to a double-blind reviewing process (i.e. reviewers do not know the identity of authors, the authors will not learn the identity of reviewers) ...

> To preserve the advantages of blind reviewing, authors should avoid self-identification in the text as well as the footnotes of their manuscripts.

In asking that an alternative form of presentation is considered by the readership of journals such as *Educational Theory*, a presentation which demands self-identification, I am conscious of entering, as Walker (1985) says, long-standing and fiercely defended positions in the history and philosophy of science. I do not enter such a debate lightly. I have found it necessary to engage with such politics of educational knowledge for the sake of developing an educational theory which can be directly related to the educational development of individuals.

The third problem is one in which the power relations in the academic community support the power of truth against the truth of power. I am thinking about the problem of testing one's ideas against those of others. In supporting the power of truth against the truth of power, academics offer their ideas for public criticism in a forum where the power of rationality in the force of better argument is paramount. Acknowledging mistakes is a fundamental part in developing our ideas.

In his paper, *Educational Theory, Practical Philosophy and Action Research*, Elliott (1987) treats Hirst (1983) rather gently and chooses a statement which does not fully acknowledge Hirst's mistake in advocating the 'disciplines approach to educational theory':

> It is not so much that what I wrote in 1966 was mistaken as that what I omitted led to a distorting emphasis. Educational theory I still see as concerned with determining rationally defensible principles for educational practice (Hirst, 1983).

Because our views about educational theory affect the way we see human existence I believe it imperative to acknowledge that mistakes have been made, and to understand the nature of these mistakes so that we can move forward.

Hirst has in fact made a most generous acknowledgement that he was mistaken in his view of educational theory:

> In many characterisations of educational theory, my own included, principles justified in this way have until recently been regarded as at best pragmatic maxims having a first crude and superficial justification in practice that in any rationally developed theory would be replaced by principles with more fundamental, theoretical, justification. That now seems to me to be a mistake (Hirst, 1983, p. 18).

I believe both Hirst and Elliott are making a mistake in their view of rationality. They both subscribe to a view of rationality which leads them to use a propositional form of discourse in their characterisations of educational theory. What I am advocating is that the propositional form of discourse in the disciplines of education should be incorporated within a living form of theory. This theory should not be seen in purely propositional terms. It should be seen to exist in the lives of practitioners as they reflect on the implications of asking themselves questions of the kind, 'How do I improve my practice?'

What I wish to do is to push Elliott's position forward. I think Gadamer points the way, but his propositional logic does not permit him to make the creative leap to a new synthesis.

Elliott points out that in developing our understanding we have to risk our values and beliefs. As we open ourselves to the things we seek to understand they will force us to become aware of problematic prejudgements and to criticise them in the light of new meanings.

Let us be clear about my purpose. I am attempting to make an acknowledged and scholarly contribution to the knowledge of my subject, education. This purpose is part of my contract of employment as a university academic. I have chosen the field of educational theory because I am committed to the profession of education and believe that it needs a theory which can adequately describe and explain the educational development of individuals. I am writing as a professional in education. In saying this I want to distinguish my activities from those of a philosopher, psychologist, sociologist or historian. I value their contributions to education but I do not believe that educational theory can be adequately characterised by any of them. I believe that philosophers, whose work I have benefited from, such as Elliott, Carr (1986) and Hirst, are limited by the propositional form of their discourse. As philosophers, rather than educationalists, they have not taken the leap necessary to comprehend the nature of educational theory. I am saying that educationalists, through studying their own attempts to answer questions such as, 'How do I improve my practice?', are constructing a living-educational-theory within which the work of Hirst, Carr, Elliott, Habermas and Gadamer is usefully integrated (Eames, 1987; Larter, 1987).

It seems to me to be crucial to ask the right questions in Collingwood's sense of moving our enquiry forward. In his work on educational theory and social change, Pritchard (1988) says that the questions are:

> How much do we wish to see? How much do we wish to understand? What conceptions, and alternative conceptions, of human practices do we have that will enable us to enhance and significantly enrich life and well-being?

Pritchard argues that we urgently need studies within educational theory which will serve to demystify institutions and to unmask ideologies. He concludes:

> It is evident that the attempt to 'raid' the disciplines of education and to use materials drawn from these areas without considerable theoretical understanding and support is ill-advised and, ultimately, is based upon an incoherent conception of the theory of education.

My worry is that Pritchard's questions are still grounded within the conceptual forms of the disciplines of education. In order to construct an educational theory for professional practice I believe we will have to face the practical and theoretical implications of asking ourselves questions of the kind, 'How do I improve my practice?'

In the past I have been critical of academics who are unwilling to study their own educational development and subject their claim to know this development to social validation (Whitehead and Foster, 1984). It seems that Whitty (1986) voices a similar criticism in the context of the work of American and Australian sociologists on the politics and sociology of education:

> Yet, if the prescriptions of these writers are not to remain purely rhetorical, there is an urgent need for them to engage in an active exploration of the implications of their work among the political constituencies in whose interests it is supposedly being carried out.

I hope to demonstrate my own engagement by investigating how relations which support the power of truth against the truth of power influence my own educational development. These influences are emerging as I engage with the politics of truth within arenas such as the educational research associations and institutions of higher education.

In conclusion I identify with a conversation between Deleuze and Foucault which considers the necessity for the practitioner of speaking on his or her own behalf:

> You were the first to teach us something absolutely fundamental: the indignity of speaking for others. We ridiculed representation and said it was finished, but we failed to draw the consequences of this 'theoretical' conversion – to appreciate the theoretical fact that only those directly concerned can speak in a practical way on their own behalf. (Foucault, 1980).

Bibliography

Argyris, C. and Schön, D. (1975) *Theory in Practice: Increasing Professional Effectiveness*. P. 5. London: Jossey-Bass.

Bayles, E.E. (1960) Are Values Verifiable? *Educational Theory*, 20; 71–78.

Bernstein, R.J. (1983) *Beyond Objectivism and Relativism*. Oxford: Basil Blackwell.

Butler, D.J. (1954) The role of value theory in educational theory. *Educational Theory*, 4; 69–77.

Carr, W. (1986) Theories of Theory and Practice. *Journal of Philosophy of Education*, 20; 177–186.

Clayton, A.S. (1969) Education and some moves towards a value methodology. *Educational Theory*, 19; 98–200.

Collingwood, R.G. (1978) *An Autobiography*. Ch. 5: Question and Answer. Oxford: Oxford University Press.

Cunningham, E.C. (1953) Extensional Limits of Aristotelian Logic. *Educational Theory*, 3; 92–10.

Eames, K. (1987) *The Growth of a Teacher-Researcher's Attempt to Understand, Writing, Redrafting, learning and Autonomy in the Examination Years*. M.Phil. dissertation. University of Bath.

Eames, K. (1988) Evaluating a Teacher Researcher's Choice of Action Research. *Assessment & Evaluation in Higher Education*, 13(3); 212–218.

Elliott, J. (1987) Educational Theory Practical Philosophy and Action Research. *British Journal of Educational Studies*, 35(2); 149–169.

Forrest, M. (1983) *The Teacher as Researcher – the use of historical artefacts in primary schools*. M.Ed. dissertation, University of Bath.

Foster, D. (1980) *Explanations for teachers' attempts to improve the process of education for their pupils*. M.Ed. dissertation, University of Bath.

Foucault, M. (1980) in C. Gordon (Ed.) *Power Knowledge*. London: Harvester.

Fromm, E. (1960) *Fear of Freedom*. p. 18. London: Routledge & Kegan Paul.

Gadamer, H.G. (1975) *Truth and Method*. London: Sheed and Ward.

Gitlin, A. and Goldstein, S. (1987) A Dialogical Approach to Understanding: Horizontal Evaluation. *Educational Theory*, 37(1); 17–29.

Habermas, J. (1976) *Communication and the Evolution of Society*. London: Heinemann.

Hirst, P.H. (Ed.) (1983) *Educational Theory and Its Foundation Disciplines*. London: Routledge.

Jensen, M. (1987) *A Creative Approach to the Teaching of English in the Examination Years*. M.Phil dissertation, University of Bath.

Kilpatrick, W. (1951) Crucial Issues in Current Educational Theory. *Educational Theory*, 1(1); 1–8.

King, R. (1987) *An Action Inquiry into Day Release in Further Education*. M.Phil dissertation, University of Bath.

Larter, A. (1985) What ought I to have done? An examination of events surrounding a racist poem. Paper to the symposium, *Action Research, Educational Theory and the Politics of Educational Knowledge,* at BERA 1985.

Larter, A. (1988) *An Action Research Approach to Classroom discussion in the Examination Years*. M.Phil dissertation, University of Bath.

Lomax, P. (1986) Action Researcher's Action Research: a BERA symposium, University of Sheffield, 30 August 1985. *British Journal of In-Service Education*, 13(1); 42–50.

Marcuse, H. (1964) *One Dimensional Man*. London: Routledge and Kegan Paul.

McNiff, J. (1988) *Action Research: Principles and Practice*. London: Macmillan.

Mosier, R.D. (1967) From Enquiry Logic to Symbolic Logic. *Educational Theory*, 17; 32–38.

Peters, R.S. (1966) *Ethics and Education*. London: Allen & Unwin.

Polanyi, M. (1958) *Personal Knowledge*. Oxford: Oxford University Press.

Popper, K. (1963) *Conjectures and Refutations*. Oxford: Oxford University Press.

Pritchard, M. (1988) Educational Theory and Social Change. *Cambridge Journal of Education*, 18(1); 99–109.

Schön, D. (1983) *The Reflective Practitioner*. New York: Basic Books.

Smith, P.G. (1976) Knowledge and Values. *Educational Theory*, 26; 29–39.

Tostberg, R.E. (1976) Observations of the Logical Bases of Educational Policy. *Educational Theory*, 26; 74–82.

Walker, R. (1985) *Doing Research*. p. 181. London: Methuen.

Whitehead, J. (1972) *A preliminary investigation of the process through which adolescents acquire scientific understanding*. Unpublished MA dissertation. University of London.

Whitehead, J. (1985) An Analysis of an Individual's Educational Development: The Basis for Personally Oriented Action Research, in *Educational Research: Principles, Policies and Practices*. Ed. Shipman, M. London: Falmer.

Whitehead, J. and Foster, D. (1984) *Action Research and professional educational development*. Cambridge Action Research Network. Bulletin No. 6, pp. 41–45.

Whitehead, J. and Lomax, P. (1987) Action Research and the Politics of Educational Knowledge. *British Educational Research Journal*, 13(2); 175–190.

Whitty, G. (1986) Recent American and Australian Approaches to the Sociology and Politics of Education: Review Article. *Educational Theory*, 36(1); 81–89.

Wittgenstein, L. (1953) *Philosophical Investigations*. Oxford: Basil Blackwell.

PAPER TWO.

Whitehead, J. (1991) How Do I Improve My Professional Practice as an Academic and Educational Manager? A Dialectical Analysis of an Individual's Educational Development and a Basis for Socially Orientated Action Research, in Collins, C. and Chippendale, P. (Eds.) *Proceedings of the First World Congress on Action Learning, Action Research and Process Management, Vol. 2*; Acorn Press. Australia.

This paper was presented in the 1990, First World Congress on Action Learning, Action Research and Process Management. It establishes a relationship between the individual and the social that grounds the question, 'How do I improve my practice?' within the social relations that help to establish my practice as an educational practice. The dialectical analysis continues to emphasise the importance, established in Paper One, of including 'I' as a living contradiction within the generation of a living-educational-theory. I examine my educational influences in my own learning as I respond to the power relations that are related to the efforts of others to terminate my employment and the success of others to protect my employment at the University of Bath. The examination also draws insights from Foucault's ideas on understanding power relations in relation to the academic legitimation of knowledge. This paper emphasises the importance of strengthening the validity of a living-educational-theory through the mutual rational controls of critical discussion (Popper, 1975, p. 44).

The dialectical analysis does not reject propositional forms of theorising with their elimination of contradictions between statements. However, I do understand, but do not agree with, Popper's (1963) reasoning for rejecting theories that contain contradictions as being entirely useless as theories. Drawing on three laws of Aristotelian logic, Popper explains why he believes that dialectical theorising is based on nothing better than a loose and woolly way of speaking (p. 316). My experience is that I exist as a living contradiction and insist on including living contradictions within my explanations of educational influence.

Whilst rejecting Popper's point about contradiction, I do integrate his idea of the mutual rational control by critical discussion into my use of validation groups to strengthen the validity of explanations of educational influences in learning. As part of these mutual rational controls, these groups also draw insights from Habermas' (1976, pp. 2–3) ideas on communication and the evolution of society, in which he explicates four criteria of social validity. I continue to use and advocate these insights up to the present day in 2018 to help in strengthening the validity of living-educational-theories.

This paper extends my educational enquiry from a personal into a social orientation with social concerns that are grounded in contradictions. The contradictions include pressures that you might have experienced yourself in resisting attempts to terminate your employment or to deny the contribution you wish to make to the organisation.

This paper is also helpful in understanding the influence of Action Research in my earlier work. It includes the inclusion of two master's units on Action Research into the professional development curriculum in the School of Education of the University of Bath. It also includes the explicit use of action-reflection cycles in moving my enquiry forward. The cycles include the expression of my concerns when my values are not being lived fully in my practice; the design of an action plan; actions that include the gathering of data to make a judgement on the effectiveness of actions; the evaluation of effectiveness and the modification of concerns, plans and actions in the light of the evaluations.

This paper also demonstrates the dominating influence of Action Research in my earlier educational enquiries before I developed an explicit awareness of the importance of including insights from Narrative Enquiry, Auto-ethnography, Phenomenology and Action Research into the generation of a living-educational-theory. These insights are included in Papers Four and Eight with their foci on methodology.

References

Popper, K. (1975) *The Logic of Scientific Discovery.* London: Hutchinson & Co.
Popper, K. (1963) *Conjectures and Refutations.* Oxford: Oxford University Press.
Habermas, J. (1976) *Communication and the Evolution of Society.* London: Heinemann.

PAPER TWO

How Do I Improve My Professional Practice as an Academic and Educational Manager? A Dialectical Analysis of an Individual's Educational Development and a Basis for Socially Orientated Action Research.

Abstract

This paper outlines a dialectical approach to educational Action Research and attempts to synthesise a process of personal development with a process of social evolution. The dialectical approach is characterised as a process of question and answer in which an individual 'I' exists as a living contradiction in questions of the kind, 'How do I improve my practice?' The potential of educational Action Research for social evolution is examined in terms of an individual's responses to contradictions in the workplace. These contradictions involve the loss of one's employment, the denial of one's originality, the denial of the right to ask questions, being disciplined for what one writes, and then having one's research legitimated in the M.Ed. curriculum of a university School of Education.

Like Critical Action Research (Carr and Kemmis, 1986) the dialectical approach will be shown to incorporate a consideration of values and power. This will be shown in two examples of Action Research and the processes of educational management. The first involves my own academic development in relation to the good order and politics of truth of a university. The second involves my contribution to the educational management of a comprehensive school. From these examples it is argued that the dialectical approach can generate valid explanations for the educational development of an individual in a way which shows that the production of a living form of educational theory from such explanations can have implications for social evolution.

Introduction

The heuristic potential of Action Research is currently being explored in a variety of forms and fields of knowledge within this congress. In the field of education, Action Research has become a major force in teachers' professional development, in educational management and educational theory. My own contribution to the field has focused on my claim to know my own educational development in the course of my enquiry, 'How do I improve the quality of my practice?' My early methodological questions progressed into epistemological enquiries related to the values, logic, units of appraisal and standards of judgement, which could be used to test claims to know the nature and processes of education (Whitehead and Foster,

1984). I became interested in trying to create a dialectical form of educational theory for producing valid explanations for the educational development of an individual (Whitehead, 1985a). My attempts to gain academic legitimacy for this dialectical approach to educational knowledge developed into questions concerning the good order and politics of truth in a university (Whitehead, 1985b). These have led to the questions in this paper concerning educational Action Research and social evolution. I want to explore with you the potential of an individual's action research, for linking educational theory and the politics of educational knowledge with social evolution, in the context of academic and institutional management.

The dialectical nature of my enquiry, 'How do I improve my practice?', can be distinguished from other approaches to Action Research as it is an attempt to answer the question of contradiction posed by Ilyenkov:

> Contradiction as the concrete unity of mutually exclusive opposites is the real nucleus of dialectics, its central category ... If any object is a 'living contradiction', what must the thought/statement about the object be that expresses it? (Ilyenkov, 1977).

In looking at videorecordings of my own teaching, I came to appreciate that 'I' existed in my question as a living contradiction in Ilyenkov's sense that I hold two mutually exclusive opposites together in practice. I could experience myself holding certain educational values, whilst at the same time denying them in my practice. For example, I could experience myself valuing my pupil's capacities to learn by enquiry whilst at the same time closing down their opportunity for doing so by the way I structured my lessons (Whitehead, 1977). I believe that the incorporation of 'I' as a living contradiction in explanations for the educational development of individuals has distinguished an original contribution to the Action Research movement by researchers associated with the School of Education of the University of Bath (Elliott, 1989; Lomax, 1989; McNiff, 1988; Whitehead, 1989). The characteristic Action Research methodology which incorporates 'I' and which has developed from this work has the form: I experience problems or concerns when some of my values are denied in my practice; I imagine ways of improving my practice and choose a course of action; I act and gather evidence which will enable me to make a judgement on the effectiveness of my actions; I evaluate the outcomes of my actions; I modify my concerns, ideas and actions in the light of my evaluation.

In analysing this claim to know my own educational development I took the unit of appraisal to be the individual's claim to know her or his own educational development. The standards of judgement I used to characterise my claim to knowledge as 'educational' included the form of the action research cycle above, Ilyenkov's criteria for characterising dialectical logic, the values defined by Peters (1966), and the aesthetic/spiritual values in Buber's characterisation of the I-You relationship (Whitehead, 1985a).

I then examined the possibility of moving from such a dialectical base into a living form of educational theory. By a 'living' theory I mean that the explanations generated by the theory to explain the educational development of individuals contain an evaluation of past practice and evidence of present practice which includes the 'I's' intention (a human goal) to produce something valued which is not yet in existence. I now claim that it is possible to construct such a theory from the explanations which individuals produce for their own educational development (Whitehead, 1989b).

My enquiry moved into the politics of truth as I encountered the power relations which legitimated the judgements, on two PhD submissions to the University of Bath. These judgements stated that I had not shown an ability to conduct original investigations or to test my own ideas or those of others, and that my work did not contain matter worthy of publication. These power relations also legitimated the instruction that under no circumstances could I question the competence of my examiners. In understanding these power relations I have used Foucault's insights into the conflict between the truth of power and the power of truth in an analysis of the procedures and rules which surround the legitimation of a dialectical claim to educational knowledge in a university.

I accept Foucault's (1977) distinction between the 'specific intellectual' as opposed to the 'universal intellectual'. He says that for a long period the 'left' intellectual was acknowledged as a champion of truth and justice. The intellectual was a spokesperson of the universal in the sense of moral, theoretical and political choices. In opposition to the universal intellectual, he describes the specific intellectual in terms of an engagement in a struggle at the precise points where their own conditions of life or work situate them. Foucault takes care to emphasise that by 'truth' he does not mean 'the ensemble of truths which are to be discovered and accepted'. By 'truth', he means the ensemble of rules according to which the true and the false are separated and specific effects of power attached to the true. The struggles 'around truth' are not 'on behalf' of the truth, but about the status of truth and the economic and political role it plays.

I am offering the following account of my struggle to support the good order and the power of truth of a university as part of my enquiry into the relationship between Action Research, educational theory, the politics of truth, and social evolution. I see this enquiry as developing from my earlier analysis of an individual's educational development which has provided the basis for personally orientated

Action Research (Whitehead, 1985b). I am now attempting to produce a basis for socially orientated Action Research which will incorporate my earlier ideas.

Extending The Educational Enquiry From A Personal Into A Social Orientation – Social Concerns Grounded In Contradictions

I wish to characterise this extension into a socially orientated Action Research by a dialogical form of presentation. This choice was influenced by Kilpatrick's (1951) point that educational theory is a form of dialogue which has profound implications for the future of humanity. I will begin to extend this social orientation by acknowledging my identification with the meanings in the following conversation between David Bohm (1988), Georg Wikman and others in which Bohm is affirming the value of originality in the perception of new meanings and relating this perception to social change:

> David Bohm: ... What actually has value would be to have a constantly creative culture. Now I suggest that such creativity is related to a constant discovery of new meanings. Generally speaking, we start from old meanings and commonly make small changes in them. Sometimes we may, however, perceive a big change of meaning. An idea changes in a fundamental way, although, of course some old features are still carried along, no matter how big the change is.
>
> Georg Wikman: But what is it that really happens when you perceive a new meaning?
>
> David Bohm: That's the creative step. If I say that meaning is being and something new is perceived in a meaning, something has changed in being. For example, all the perceptions that took place in science changed the meaning of the world for us and this changed the world. It first changed in the sense that we saw it differently: but science also changed the physical, the somatic level. The entire earth has been changed and it could have changed a lot more, for the better or for the worse. Therefore, at least in my own experience, being and meaning are there together.
>
> And I'm proposing this more generally. So if somebody sees a different meaning to society or to life, that will change society. Every revolution has come from somebody seeing a different meaning in human society. For example, the meaning that some people saw was that of a very static society, where everybody was in his place and the top was overlooking the bottom. Then other people saw a different meaning, according to which people should be equal. That different meaning was the power that generated the change. (Pylkkänen, 1989).

The new meaning I am seeking to share is in showing what it means for individual researchers to speak on their own behalf as they attempt to transcend the truth of power through the power of truth in their workplace. This meaning is extended in the second enquiry as I explore the nature of educative relationships within the power of truth. I argue that 'educational' researchers who are making claims to educational and professional knowledge should be showing how they are enabling the professionals and their pupils and students to speak on their own behalf. It is the idea that researchers should be showing what it means for themselves to be living more fully their values in their workplace and showing how they are enabling the 'researched' to speak on their own behalf which I am offering as a basis for socially orientated, educational Action Research.

As a dialectician, who is interested in moving understanding forward through a process of question and answer, I accept the category of contradiction as the nucleus of dialectics. I also believe that social change and transformation can be understood in terms of the attempts by human beings to resolve their consciously lived contradictions. Because of these assumptions I will begin with the five experiences of contradiction which have moved me into the present phase of my enquiry. I am hoping that you will identify with these contradictions and my responses in the sense that they raise fundamental questions about human existence. I am thinking of questions concerning the appropriate response to: being sacked; having one's originality and the right to ask questions denied; being told that one's research and teaching were inconsistent with one's duties to the employer; being asked to teach a curriculum based upon the research and writings which were at the focus of the earlier contradictions.

Whilst these contradictions are socially and historically located within a particular time and culture, I am interested in exploring the potential significance of the ensuing actions for social evolution. What I have in mind is the possibility that you will identify with the experience of the truth of power which denies the individual the right to practise his or her vocation; which denies the individual the right to ask questions; which refuses to acknowledge the individual's contribution to knowledge; which mobilises other power relations to try to prevent the individual teaching and researching a chosen area. I think you will identify with these experiences in the historical sense that many other individuals have been subjected to such power relations and that the course of social evolution can partly be understood in terms of the responses which individuals and groups have made to these experiences of oppression. In my own case I am hoping that you will identify with my responses to the following contradictions in the sense that you will feel moved by them to help to generate a living form of educational theory which has implications for social evolution through its goal of human betterment.

Holding Together the Academic Vocation and Having One's Employment Terminated

The first major contradiction I had to come to terms with involved both my economic well-being and my sense of vocation to make a contribution to the reconstruction of educational theory through my work in the university. Being informed that my employment was terminated meant that I experienced the contradiction of holding together my sense of vocation together with the denial of my sense of vocation in the grounds given below to sack me. The grounds given for terminating my employment were:

> The Academic Staff Committee's grounds for recommending that a new appointment should not be offered are as follows:
>
> 1. That you have not given satisfaction in the teaching of prescribed courses assigned to you.
>
> 2. That there is an absence of evidence to suggest that you have pursued research of sufficient quality for the assessors to be assured of your ability to perform adequately the duties of a University Lecturer; the objectives being to make acknowledged scholarly contributions to the advancement of your subject as well as to perform proper teaching and other administrative tasks.
>
> 3. That you have exhibited forms of behaviour which have harmed the good order and morale of the School of Education.

The power behind these judgements was reinforced by their acceptance by the university Senate. Given the force of the judgements I think you will appreciate how much energy and commitment were required to overthrow them. I owe my existence as a tenured academic of the university to the commitment, values, actions and political and legal understandings of other individuals both within and outside the university (Whitehead, 1985b). I simply wish to share this insight with you as an acknowledgement that my past and future contributions to education, in the university, are grounded in those individuals who refused to accept the above judgements on my work. Because they engaged in the necessary political activities they overcame the power relations which were attempting to sustain these judgements. In recognition of their ethical and political commitments I could not in future jeopardise this tenure in the quest for promotion in the University of Bath. In the university promotion is now accompanied by a loss of tenure.

Holding Together Originality and the Right to Ask Questions with their Denial.

The second and third contradictions are focused on my failure to gain academic legitimacy for two PhD theses I submitted to the university in 1980 and 1982 entitled, respectively, 'Educational Practice and its Theory' and 'A Dialectical Approach to Education'. The second contradiction is grounded in the denial of my originality by the university's examiners and Board of Studies for Education. I am thinking of my claim to originality in my decision to ground my understanding of the world within personal knowledge (Polanyi, 1959). The ability to make original contributions to one's subject is traditionally respected in academic life. These original contributions are often submitted for PhD examination in which examiners are asked to judge the originality of the text. When my examiners were asked the question as to whether I had demonstrated an ability to conduct original investigations, to test my own ideas and those of others, they claimed that I had not shown such an ability.

These judgements were accepted by the Board of Studies for Education and my appeal against these judgements was rejected by the Board of Studies in November 1980. My approach to overcoming this contradiction has been a public one. I have great faith in the truth-seeking capacities of human beings. That is why I believe I must subject my claims of originality to public test in contexts such as this World Congress. Just as I have faith in our truth-seeking capacities, I have faith that our creativity and originality together with our critical abilities will move our ideas forward. In time you will be able to judge whether I have shown an ability to conduct original investigations, to test my own ideas and those of others, or whether my examiners were correct in denying that I had shown these abilities. Whether you make your own judgements public is up to you. The third contradiction was grounded in a judgement on the University Regulations that once examiners had been appointed by the Senate under no circumstances could their competence be questioned. Given that I wished to question the competence of my examiners on the grounds of political bias, prejudice and inadequate assessment I had to hold such questioning together with the force of an instruction from the university that under no circumstances could I question their competence.

I overcame this contradiction on 1 June 1990 with a presentation to a research seminar at the Centre for the Study of Management Learning at Lancaster University (Whitehead, 1990). I outlined my arguments for demanding the right to question the competence of my examiners on the grounds of bias, prejudice and inadequate assessment. In presenting the evidence which I believe would convince any rational individual that there is a case to answer I felt protected by the law which guarantees my academic freedom to ask questions.

Holding Together the Power of Truth and the Truth of Power

I experienced my fourth contradiction on 1 May 1987 when I attended a meeting held under the authority of the University Council to hear complaints about my activities and writings which had been made to the university by two Professors of Education. I was in no doubt that my activities and writings were being viewed as incompatible with the duties the university wished me to pursue in teaching and research. I was thus faced with holding together my support for the power of truth in researching the politics of truth within my University together with the truth of power within the university which was attempting to block this research.

Holding Together the Acceptance of my Research in the School's Curriculum with the Above Contradictions

I experienced my fifth contradiction at the Board of Studies of Education on 9 May 1990 when the Board agreed to send to Senate two proposals on action research modules for the M.Ed. programme – the highest level of taught course in the School of Education. The upsurge of interest in Action Research approaches to professional development had convinced the majority of staff in the School of Education that we should offer taught courses on Action Research. These modules, whilst drawing on the work of other academics, clearly reference my research and writings over my seventeen years in the university. Hence, I was faced with the experience of contradiction of holding together the experience of the Board of Studies legitimating my research and writings in the taught M.Ed. programme with the experience of the University's and Board of Studies' denial of the legitimacy of this knowledge in previous judgements on my research. So, I am in the position of being asked to teach a curriculum which includes references to the activities, writings, teaching and research whose legitimacy has been denied in judgements which are still in force.

Moving The Enquiry Forward

The fourth and fifth contradictions are related and I will now outline the action cycle I am using to resolve these contradictions by moving my enquiry forward into the good order and politics of truth within the university. What I mean by good order is related to the values of the Academic Assembly of the university:

> High sounding phrases like 'values of freedom, truth and democracy', 'rational debate', 'integrity', have been used. It is easy to be cynical about these and to dismiss them as hopelessly idealistic, but without ideals and a certain agreement about shared values a community cannot be sustained, and will degenerate. These are the phrases in which members of Academic Assembly have chosen to convey

their concept of this community. (The Idea of a University. Academic Assembly, University of Bath, 1988).

The Statutes of the University enable Academic Assembly to remain a democratic forum to discuss any matter of concern to the University and to pass resolutions to Senate. It is this capacity to support the power of truth against the truth of power through dialogue and democratic decision-making which has focused my attention on the value of Academic Assembly in sustaining and promoting the good order of the university. Given this context, my next question is: Can I relate Action Research to social evolution through an analysis of an individual's educational development? I think Foucault (1980) points the way to answer this question through his idea that as a university academic I occupy a specific position in the economy which is linked to the politics of truth within our society. If I use this idea to show how I am changing power relations which are related to that regime of truth which is essential to the structure and functioning of our society and our world, have I not established the practical principle that this individual's actions can be related to social evolution?

My question is related to Bohm's earlier point about a constantly creative culture. I am trying to show what it means for an academic to try to constitute a 'good' order in his workplace through giving a new meaning to the relationship between the power of truth and the truth of power – a meaning which is part of the process of transcending the truth of power through the power of truth. I think my proposals for a socially orientated educational Action Research rests on the extent to which you identify these contradictions as intrinsic to the power relations in your own societies and forms of life.

I claim that these contradictions can be understood in terms of a conflict between the power of truth and the truth of power. At one pole of the contradictions in my workplace is the power of truth in the values embodied by the Academic Assembly. At the other pole of the contradiction are the negations of these values in judgements which have been upheld by the truth of power of the University Council, Senate and a Board of Studies. I thus see my educational development in the good order and politics of truth in the university as an examination of what it takes to move the power of truth into an ascendancy over the truth of power. I propose to try to achieve this through public debate and dialogue within the above bodies and in contexts such as this, outside the university.

I want to make a distinction between Action Research and educational Action Research in terms of values. If Action Research is characterised by a particular form of systematic enquiry then there is no necessity to justify the value base of the enquiry in defining the research as 'Action Research'. Action Research could, in these terms, be used to increase the efficiency of activities which could be morally unacceptable. In claiming that my research is 'educational' I am committing myself to upholding the values of good order. I am not willing to accept the term 'educational' to describe activities which are undermining these values.

In undertaking educational Action Research I accept the responsibility of making public the values which I use to characterise my activities as 'educational'. In showing what it means for an individual's educational development to try to live by the values which are embodied in the Academic Assembly's notion of good order and in trying to ensure the ascendancy of the power of truth over the truth of power, I am attempting to establish a basis for a socially orientated, educational Action Research.

I am not restricting my view of 'educational development' to the traditional view of educational institutions such as schools, colleges, polytechnics and universities. I see any development in which individuals are learning what it means to live more fully their values in their practice as potentially 'educational'. The generality of my account and hence its relationship to social evolution rest upon the way in which others identify their contradictions with my own and find it useful in making sense of their own lives in their own action enquiry in the workplace.

The kind of enquiry I have in mind is like the first one below in which I move from an examination of the concerns created by the experience of contradiction, to the design of an action plan, to acting, evaluating and modifying concerns, plans and actions.

I now want to present the evidence of the development of my latest action cycles. The first concerns the educational management of my own learning in the good order and politics of truth within the University of Bath. The second presents evidence from my enquiry, 'How do I improve the quality of my contribution to the educational management of a comprehensive school?' The evidence demonstrates my support for the introduction of an Action Research approach to professional development with its commitment to democratic procedures within the school. I want to use the second example to illustrate a point about the nature of educative relationships which I believe will challenge the validity of the propositional writings of many 'educational' researchers particularly those researching the professional learning of teachers. At the end of each enquiry I will briefly review how I see the present position.

Constructing an Action Plan and Acting

The experiences of the contradictions and conflicts discussed above led me to submit a paper to the Secretary of the Board of Studies of the School of Education, under an item dealing with the Good Order of the School of Education, for a meeting on 9 May 1990. I wished to raise the issues concerning the above contradictions in relation to the organisation and curriculum of the school. The Head of the School of Education sought the advice of the Secretary and Registrar who ruled that the matter was not appropriate business for the Board of Studies.

Evaluation and Modified Plan

This rejection was followed by a discussion with the Head of School. My evaluation was that, if I was to set out my reasons for believing that the item was appropriate matter, under the University Statutes, for consideration by the Board of Studies, then the rationality of my case would convince him to include it on the agenda. This led me to respond with the reasons why I believed that the matter was appropriate for the Board of Studies and why I believed the matter was related to the good order of the School of Education in relation to the University Statutes. The Head of School is responsible to the Vice-Chancellor for the good order of the School of Education and my response was based on my feeling that I had not communicated my intentions clearly enough. I was seeking to place material before the Board of Studies which would reveal fundamental contradictions in its judgements relating to the organisation of teaching, research and the curricula of the school. I was also trying to explain how such contradictions have arisen and what might be done to resolve them. At its meeting on 20 June 1990, the Board decided that it should discuss the issue and that I could now submit my material to the next meeting in October 1990.

I also locate my understanding of the value of academic freedom in relation to the politics of truth, in the context of the invitation to present a paper on my research to this congress. Following complaints made by two Professors of Education about my activities and writings at the hearing on 1 May 1987, the University required me to submit such papers to the Head of School before publication so that I might be told if I am prejudicing the University's relationships. I have submitted this paper to the Head of School in the context of the Education Reform Act which states that:

> ... academic staff have freedom within the law to question and test received wisdom, and to put forward new ideas and controversial or unpopular opinions, without placing themselves in jeopardy of losing their jobs or privileges they may have at their institutions.

Criteria for Judging Effectiveness

In the design of an action plan I always encourage my students to include the details of the kind of evidence they would need to enable them to make a judgement on their effectiveness. I also encourage them to make explicit the criteria on which these judgements are based. I will make a similar demand of myself evaluating the effectiveness of my actions. I would expect to see my research papers showing a developing understanding of an individual's educational development in relation to the good order and politics of truth in a university. In making judgements with universal intent I judge my effectiveness in terms of the extent to which my ideas are useful to others in their attempts to make sense of their own educational practice. If my questioning is fundamental and we experience ourselves as existing in more creative rather than hostile cultures, then I would expect others to participate in the creation of a public living-educational-theory which could be shown to have profound implications for the future of humanity (Kilpatrick, 1951). I believe that this will occur as we explore and share what it means for our educational development as we live more fully the values of freedom, truth, democracy, rational debate and integrity in our workplace and world, and create a living-educational-theory through dialogue.

In evaluating my past practice I am aware of the social relations which protected my job, when my employment was terminated in 1976, and the social relations implicit in my use of the ideas of others in making sense of my own life. For example, I owe my ability to articulate my decision to understand the world from my own point of view as a person claiming originality and exercising his judgement with universal intent to Polanyi's (1959) insights into the grounds of personal knowledge. I use this insight in defining the unit of appraisal in my claim to educational knowledge. I take the unit to be an individual's claim to know her or his own educational development. In developing my understanding of the implications of the standards of judgement I use in testing my claims to educational knowledge for social evolution, I have been influenced by Habermas' views in communication and the evolution of society. I accept Habermas' (1976) point that the validity claims I am making in my attempt to communicate can be judged in terms of coherence, values, truth and authenticity (Whitehead, 1989b). When I consider the validity of my claims to educational knowledge I also draw upon MacIntyre's (1988) insight that the rival claims to truth of contending traditions of enquiry depend for their vindication upon the adequacy and the explanatory power of the histories which the resources of each of those traditions in conflict enable their adherents to write. I thus see the extension of my enquiry into questions concerning social evolution to be related to the grounds of my judgements in personal knowledge in that the judgements are being made responsibly with universal intent.

In addition to these points concerning validity I am interested in developing an understanding of an appropriate concept of rigour for Action Research. Winter

(1989) has proposed six principles for the rigorous conduct of Action Research which he refers to as: Reflexive and Dialectical Critique; Collaborative Resource; Risk; Plurality of Structure and Theory; Practice; Transformation. These principles, whilst open to refinement, for example in the understanding of the values which are required to conduct a rigorous form of educational Action Research, are the principles which I accept as appropriate for judging the rigour of my own enquiry.

I now want to move the context of my enquiry from the educational management of my professional development as an academic researcher into the context of my contribution to the educational management of a comprehensive school. I have shown what it means for a dialectical Action Researcher to speak on his own behalf. I now want to show what it means to engage in a dialectical form of Action Research in which one's professional colleagues are being encouraged to develop democratic forms of decision-making and being enabled to speak, in the research, on their own behalf.

Dialectical Action Research In The Social Context Of A School

I now want to extend my action enquiry into the social base of a secondary school through answering the question, 'How do I improve my contribution to the educational management of a Comprehensive School through my activities as Chair of Governors?'

Concern

In particular I want to focus on the values of rationality and democracy and present the evidence to show how I am trying to embody these values in my form of life. Following on from my previous analysis, I want to show what it means for me to be engaged in Action Research in which the power of truth is in the ascendancy over the truth of power. I want to do this by showing what it means to empower a teacher to speak on his own behalf rather than for me, as a researcher, to make a claim to knowledge about the professional learning of teachers without enabling teachers to speak for themselves. In judging my efforts to improve the quality of my contribution to the educational management of a secondary school I wish to focus on the value of rationality as it is embodied in the action research cycle and the value of democratic procedures in staff selection.

I will relate my enquiry to the evidence provided by the acting head of the school in relation to the acceptance of an Action Research approach to professional development and to the first democratic election for a staff development tutor. The extracts from the school's and the Local Education Authority's (LEA) policy documents below show that I have moved my contribution from a position where I was part of a management structure supporting forms of professional development which did not incorporate the above view of rationality, to a position which supported the above view of rationality in the way described below.

Actions

Over the past four years Avon LEA has paid the University of Bath a consultancy fee to enable me to spend some time promoting Action Research with teachers. In March 1990 Avon LEA published a booklet on 'You and Your Professional Development', which commits the Authority to providing the majority of its INSET (Inservice Education of Teachers) support through an Action Research approach to professional development.

The following extracts from a paper from the Acting Head of the School to the Senior Management Team dated 5 March 1990 show clearly the integration of an Action Research approach into the School's policy for staff development for 1990–91:

> We have for a long time at Culverhay been very concerned about an INSET Policy which requires teachers to LEAVE their classes with a supply teacher, often with no expertise in the subject area, and for understandable reasons without the same commitment to the progress of the pupils.

> The advantage to the School of teachers engaged in this form of INSET is also questionable, although we have tried to reduce the problems of 'cascading' by having a 'reporting back' form, which is then circulated to the relevant members of staff.

> From the LEA draft Staff Development Policy, it is clear that INSET should now be much more CLASSROOM-based, and resources should be allocated to support teachers as they carry out their work. Several Culverhay Staff have been involved in such INSET/STAFF DEVELOPMENT over the last few years, and the most recent example was the STRICT initiative (Supporting Teacher Research Into Classroom Teaching).

> Staff are gaining experience in 'action research' techniques, which basically follows the pattern shown below:

> 1. The teacher identifies or is presented with a problem, and chooses a colleague to work with to help find a solution.

> 2. The teacher works with the colleague both inside and outside the classroom, with the aim of devising an approach which will improve the quality of education provided.

3. The lesson is taught, and information collected as the class proceeds which will highlight whether or not the approach is a successful one.

4. Following the class, the lesson is assessed by the two teachers.

5. The next stage requires a new, improved approach to the topic to be devised, building on the experience gained from the research.

Thus the cycle of events can be continued, with both colleagues benefiting professionally from the experience, and the quality of the classroom teaching hopefully improving as a result.

The following extract from the Acting Head shows my own commitment to the democratic principle of staff selecting their own staff development tutor:

We have been asked by the LEA to appoint a Staff Development Tutor. This position should be assessed annually. The role/qualities of this person are outlined below:

1. The Staff Development Tutor (S.D.T.) will be required to help staff decide on which aspects of their classroom work they wish to develop through Action Research.

2. The S.D.T., to be effective, needs to be accepted by his or her colleagues as equal partners. He or she needs to be able to work alongside teachers in an open and supportive way. The Chair of Governors and I are both happy to see the Staff select and appoint an S.D.T. for 1990–91 (School Policy document 20/4/90).

Evaluation

My claim to be improving my contribution to the educational management of Culverhay School rests upon the evidence of the integration of an Action Research approach to professional development in the school's policy and practices. It was grounded in my view of the rationality of Action Research as an approach to improving the quality of education with teachers and pupils and the support for the extension of democratic practices in the workplace. The latter was exemplified in the process of staff selection of their own Staff Development Tutor.

I want to emphasise that the evidence I have presented for my claim to be contributing to improvements in educational management of a school, was provided in the writings of a teacher. These were not my words; they were his. In seeing my contribution to educational management as a form of educative relationship I think my claims to educational knowledge of such relationships rest upon the acknowledgement by others of the value they have found in my activities, research and writings.

Modified Plans

On 26 June 1990 the local authority agreed to fund a curriculum innovation on technical and vocational education in the school. The teaching and learning styles favoured by this innovation are similar to the form of action cycle described above. My plans are to support the development of a school-based Action Research group to help the teachers to answer questions of the kind, 'How do I improve my practice?', in relation to this innovation. I will be helping to gather evidence and to evaluate the practitioners' research reports in an attempt to see if it is possible to produce reports in which both the pupils and the teachers are speaking on their own behalf. I would like to extend this idea of 'speaking on your own behalf' into 'educational' research in general, by asking a number of questions of my professional and academic colleagues.

In submitting my ideas for your criticism, I am conscious of the vulnerability which comes from an openness to change because one recognises failure and error. I want you to recognise an original contribution to educational research. I may not receive such recognition because you may rightly refuse this acknowledgement. I trust that your acknowledgements or refusals will rest upon the power of your rational criticism in support of the power of truth, and that you will present your criticisms openly and in a public arena.

In presenting my ideas in the above form I am conscious that it may contain an implicit criticism of your own ideas. I am thinking of those of you who claim to belong to an educational research community and who, whilst believing that your research is 'educational', do not show what your research means for your own or others' educational practice. I am addressing the following points and questions to all those who believe that their research is 'educational research'.

Further Questions

I am assuming that we share the conviction that it was right to abandon the disciplines approach to educational research (dominant in the 1960s and 1970s) because it was both mistaken (Hirst, 1983) and, by virtue of the ideological power of its proponents, exercising a damaging influence on the views of teachers and academics. The power of criticisms from critical theorists and others helped to create a climate in which alternative views began to emerge. My worry is that the alternatives (such as Critical Theory) have replaced the ideological hegemony of the disciplines approach with the hegemony of your own critical/interpretative and thus propositional forms which are clearly identified through their organising concepts as a philosophy of education (Carr, 1989; Carr and Kemmis, 1986; Rudduck, 1989), a sociology of education (Whitty, 1986) a history of education (Hamilton, 1989, 1990) and a psychology of education (Calderhead, 1988).

I recognise these texts as having value for my educational discourse but they contain no synthesis which enables education to be viewed in a way which is holistic and dynamic. If you believe your research to be 'educational', in whose sense is it 'educational'? Can you substantiate a claim to be 'educational researchers' without an examination of your own or another's educational development? I am hoping that you will respond to my questions in a way which can help to establish a personal and social basis for educational Action Research and help to create a living-educational-theory which may indeed have 'profound implications for the future of humanity'. In asking such questions I am wondering if you experience contradictions in your workplace. Watkins (1987) in his research on the contested workplace has argued that:

> ...during work experience the contradictions of work are exposed and thus may serve to undermine the existing social relations of work by revealing both the oppositional forms and the stark 'reality' of the workplace.

As well as conducting research on students, I wonder whether such researchers have a responsibility to conduct research on themselves in their own workplace as they show what it means for their educational development to live more fully their values in their practice.

My questions concerning the potential of Action Research and educational theory for social evolution have emerged from my recognition of the power relations which protected my job in the university and in the legal protection given to me as an academic by the Education Reform Act of 1988. This act protects my right to question freely and to test received wisdom. It also protects the freedom of academics to put forward new ideas and controversial and unpopular opinions, without placing themselves in jeopardy of losing their jobs or privileges they may have at their institutions.

In offering a case study of an individual's educational development and questioning its relationship to social evolution, I am opening myself once again to criticism. I am thinking of the charges of arrogance, of making ridiculous and unsubstantiated claims, of trying to claim a potential for Action Research which it does not have, or of being incomprehensible from the Deakin point of view! I may indeed be mistaken. Yet of all the criteria I have mentioned in this paper for judging its validity I wish to return to Habermas' criteria of authenticity where he says that it is only through watching a person through time, in action, that we will be able to judge that person's authenticity. I must leave you to judge freely and wisely in the hope that you will feel moved to go public on your judgements on my research. I hope that you will do this within a dialogue which shows how you are trying to live more fully your educational values in your workplace as you support the power of truth against the truth of power. In this way, as I have argued, will you not be making your own contribution to the evolution of our society through education?

Acknowledgements

In producing this paper I have benefited from the advice and criticism of colleagues in the School of Education and local teachers. In particular my thanks to James Calderhead, Mary Tasker, Cyril Selmes, Chris James, Cecelia Higman, Joan Whitehead, Moira Laidlaw, Peter Watkins and Jane Raybould.

****

In the summer of 1990, after some difficulties about whether the item could be considered by the Board of Studies for Education I managed to submit the letter I had received from the Secretary and Registrar in June 1987 for consideration by the Board. As a result, a Senate working party was established to look into a claim that there was prima facie evidence that my academic freedom had been constrained. For the fourth time I am asking you to identify with an important learning experience in the workplace. The recognition by some colleagues that the reason that my academic freedom had not been breached was because of my persistence in the face of pressure and that a less determined individual might well have been discouraged and therefore constrained does at least have the merit of an acknowledgement that I been subjected to pressure!

References

Avon, LEA. (1990) *You and Your Professional Development*. Avon Education Authority, England.

Bohm, D. and Peat, D. (1989) *Science Order and Creativity*. London: Routledge.

Briggs, J. and McCluskey, F. (1989) Ultimate Questeners: The Search for "Omnivalent Meaning", in Pylkkänen, P., ibid p. 280.

Calderhead, J. (1988) *The Professional Learning of Teachers*. London: Falmer.

Carr, W. (1990) *The Quality of Teaching*. London: Falmer.

Carr, W. and Kemmis, S. (1986) *Becoming Critical: Education, Knowledge and Action Research*. London: Falmer.

Elliott, J. (1989) The Professional Learning of Teachers. *Cambridge Journal of Education*, 19; 81–101.

Foucault, M. (1977) Intellectuals and Power – A conversation between Michel Foucault and Gilles Deleuze: in *Michel Foucault: Language, Counter-memory, Practice*, Bouchard, D.F. (Ed.), Oxford: Basil Blackwell.

Foucault, M. (1980) in C. Gordon (Ed.) *Power Knowledge*. London: Harvester.

Habermas, J. (1976) *Communication and the Evolution of Society*. London: Routledge.

Hamilton, D. (1989) *Towards a Theory of Schooling*. London: Falmer.

Hamilton, D. (1990) *Learning About Education: An Unfinished Curriculum*. England: Open University Press.

Hirst, P. (Ed.) (1983) *Educational Theory and Its Foundation Disciplines*. London: Routledge.

Ilyenkov, E. (1977) *Dialectical Logic*. Moscow: Progress.

Kilpatrick, W.H. (1951) Crucial Issues in Current Educational Theory. *Educational Theory*, 1; 1–8.

Lomax, P. (1989) *The Management of Change*. Clevedon: Multilingual Matters.

MacIntyre, A. (1988) *Whose Justice? Which Rationality?* London: Duckworth.

McNiff, J. (1988) *Action Research: Principles and Practice*. London: Macmillan.

Peters, R.S. (1966) *Ethics and Education*. London: Allen & Unwin.

Polanyi, M. (1959) *Personal Knowledge*. London: Routledge and Kegan Paul.

Pylkkänen, P. (Ed.) (1989) *The Search for Meaning: The New Spirit in Science and Philosophy*. England: Crucible.

Rudduck, J. (1989) Practitioner Research and Programmes of Initial Teacher Education. *Westminster Studies in Education*, 12; 61–72.

Watkins, P. (1987) Student participant-observation in the contested workplace: the policy dilemmas of in-school work experience. *Journal of Education Policy*, 2; 27–42.

Whitehead, J. (1977) The Process of improving education within schools, paper to the 1977 Annual Conference of the British Educational Research Association.

Whitehead, J. (1985a) The analysis of an individual's educational development: in Shipman, M. (Ed.), *Educational Research: Principles, Policies & Practice*. London: Falmer.

Whitehead, J. (1985b) The logic of educational knowledge. Paper to BERA '85. University of Sheffield.

Whitehead, J. (1989a) Creating a Living Educational Theory from Questions of the Kind, 'How do I Improve my Practice?' *Cambridge Journal of Education*, 19; 41–52.

Whitehead, J. (1989b) How do we Improve Research-based Professionalism in Education – A question which includes action research, educational theory and the politics of educational knowledge? *British Educational Research Journal*, 15; 3–17.

Whitehead and Foster, D. (1984) *Action Research and Professional Development*. Bulletin No. 6 of the Classroom Action Research Network, University of East Anglia.

Whitty, G. (1986) Recent American and Australian approaches to the sociology and politics of education: review article. *Educational Theory*, 36; 81–89.

Winter, R. (1990) *Learning from Experience*. England: Falmer.

PAPER THREE.

How Valid are Multi-Media Communications of my Embodied Values in Living Theories and Standards of Educational Judgement and Practice? **Paper presented at the 2002 conference of the American Educational Research Association in New Orleans.**

Educational theories have been communicated through printed texts that conform to a language and logic that dominates the epistemology in Western academies (de Sousa Santos, 2014). Since 1972, when I was asked to explore the educational potential of video in the science department of Erkenwald Comprehensive School in London, I have used visual data to clarify meanings of embodied expressions of values, and I have included this data in evidence-based explanations of educational influence. In 2003 I was a member of a working party established by the Senate of the University of Bath to review the regulations governing the submission of research degrees. The regulations in 2003 did not permit the submission of e-media. A recommendation from the working party to permit the submission of e-media in research degrees was accepted by Senate, and this was enacted in 2004. The technological advance of digital video has enabled the method of empathetic resonance to be used to clarify meanings of embodied expressions of ontological and relational values. I give more details of this method in Paper Five.

Much has been done by behavioural psychologists to analyse behaviour using various forms of coding. This use of digital data in a living-theory is different to that from a coding or category system. In Living Theory research digital data is used as evidence in a values-based explanation of educational influences in learning.

Paper Three justifies a claim concerning the validity of multimedia communications of embodied values in living-theories and standards of educational judgement and practice. In this 2002 paper I use lengthy video clips to document doctoral supervision relationships and to demonstrate learning over time. This is a different use of digital video data to where I use short clips, with empathetic resonance, to clarify and communicate the meanings of embodied expressions of values.

PAPER THREE.

How Valid are Multi-Media Communications of my Embodied Values in Living Theories and Standards of Educational Judgement and Practice?

Summary

The upsurge of interest in Self-Study, Action Research and practitioner-research has led to calls by educational researchers for agreed-upon procedures for transforming knowledge based on personal experiences of practice into 'public' knowledge (Snow, 2001). As education is a value-laden practical activity, this will require a transformation of values into communicable standards of judgement for publicly testing the validity of educational knowledge-claims.

This paper shows the procedure through which a practitioner-researcher can use multimedia data from practice to transform values into communicable and living standards of judgement. It goes on to show how the standards of originality of mind and critical judgement can be used to test the validity of his claims to know his educative influence in student learning.

This paper also answers the criticism (Noffke, 1997) that theories from self-study research seem incapable of addressing issues of power of privilege in society

Introduction

Inspiration for this break with my traditional, text-based presentations comes from a range of sources. One was Elliot Eisner's (1993) presidential address to AERA in 1993 where he called for and used a multimedia presentation of alternative forms of data representation in educational research. Another was Maura McIntyre and Ardra Cole's (2001) performance text at the Third International Conference of the Self-Study of Teacher Education Practices Special Interest Group of AERA. There was also the inspiration of seeing Marian Naidoo presenting a 'performance text' (Mills, 2000, pp. 132–135) on the care of Alzheimer's patients to a group of practitioner-researchers at Bath.

Because this paper seeks to characterise contributions to educational knowledge in terms of 'living standards of judgement' I will begin by distinguishing between 'spectator' and 'living truth'. To avoid the unnecessary repetition of 'educational' throughout the paper I am assuming it as a prefix when I use the words influence, judgement, values, knowledge, and theory:

> Existentialists such as Gabriel Marcel (cf. Keen, 1966) distinguish between "spectator" truth and "living" truth. The former is generated by disciplines (e.g.

experimental science, psychology, sociology) which rationalise reality and impose on it a framework which helps them to understand it, but at the expense of oversimplifying it. Such general explanations can be achieved only by standing back from and "spectating" the human condition from a distance, as it were, and by concentrating on generalities and ignoring particularities which do not fit the picture. Whilst such a process is very valuable, it is also very limited because it is one step removed from reality. The "living" "authentic" truth of a situation can be fully understood only from within the situation though the picture that emerges will never be as clear-cut as that provided by "spectator" truth. (Burke, 1992, p. 222).

The enquiries below include insights from the 'spectator' and 'living' truths of others. Some researchers may also find unusual my use of 'I' in scholarly discourse. However, I am hoping that first-person research is now sufficiently well established in the Academy (Zeichner, 1999; McNiff, 2000a; Whitehead, 2000a) to require no further justification in terms of its legitimacy. I want to be careful here because of a difference I see between legitimacy and validity. Legitimacy in particular contexts appears to depend on the power relations that sustain procedures for defining what counts as knowledge. Legitimacy may only have weak connections with validity in the sense of a knowledge-claim that can be tested for validity using appropriate standards of judgement. So, in relation to legitimacy, Galileo could be shown instruments of torture as if they were to be used to make him retract a belief he knew to be true. The belief that the earth was the centre of the universe and that the sun revolved around the earth continued to be legitimated by the Catholic Church when the belief lacked validity.

The fact that some beliefs are held to be legitimate through procedures sustained by particular power relations does not mean they are valid. Validity depends upon the capacity to test the beliefs with standards of judgement. Hence my interest in this paper of defining standards of judgement by clarifying the meanings of my embodied values as these meanings emerge through practice. I have chosen to focus on my values of originality of mind and critical judgement in relation to my educative influence because they have personal, professional and social significance. They are personally and professionally significant because they are at the centre of my view of education. For me to accept something as educational it must involve someone learning something of value in a way that has engaged their originality of mind and critical judgement. They are socially significant in the context of my work in the University of Bath, because every PhD thesis is assessed by examiners with these standards of judgement. The importance of such standards is that their meanings can be publicly shared and hence used to test the validity of claims to knowledge.

The process of clarifying the meanings of values and transforming them into standards of judgement involves both ostensive and lexical definitions. In the ostensive definitions shown below, experiential meanings of embodied values are linked to the words 'originality of mind' and 'critical judgement' through pointing to the video images, which show the meanings emerging through practice. These ostensive definitions are supplemented by lexical definitions in which words are defined in terms in other words. It is claimed below that this process of clarification transforms the meanings of embodied values of originality of mind and critical judgement in relation to educative influence into communicable standards of judgement. I will show how these standards can be used to test the validity of a claim to know my educational influence in another researcher's explanation for her 'systems' influence as she researches her practice as a Superintendent of Schools.

I first want to see if I can establish with you a shared understanding of standards of judgement. As educational standards are necessarily value-laden it is important to check the extent to which an intersubjective agreement can be established about the meanings of embodied values and their use as standards of judgement. If standards are to be 'educational' it is important to understand that they, too, are living and open to change and transformation (Laidlaw, 1996).

Clarifying The Meanings Of Embodied Values Using Video Clips From The Researchers' Practice And Testing The Validity Of These Meanings As Standards Of Judgement.

I want to begin by showing you what I do in my educative relations and asking 'what am I doing?' This beginning relates to an epistemological principle in the phenomenology of Husserl (1931). Like me, you may find Husserl expresses himself in complex language that is difficult to understand. However, because the following principle has profoundly influenced my own epistemology, I want to acknowledge its significance. Husserl says that in the transcendental sphere there is an infinitude of knowledge previous to all deduction, knowledge whose mediated connections of intentional implication have nothing to do with deduction. He says that this knowledge, being entirely intuitive, proves refractory to 'every methodologically devised scheme of constructive symbolism' (p. 12). By this I take him to mean that this knowledge requires accessing in ways that cannot fit within predefined or analytic category systems.

The influence of Husserl's original formulation can be seen in my own view that in what I am doing there is an infinitude of knowledge previous to all deduction. This knowledge is embodied in practice and is in what you can see me doing. Hence I want to begin with the following video clip because it shows you what I am doing in supervising a PhD researcher as I am asking, 'How can I help you to improve your learning?' I will return to the clip below, together with a transcript from the video, in an analysis of my influence.

The context of this first video clip and enquiry is my supervision of Jackie Delong's doctoral research. Jackie is a Superintendent of Schools in Ontario. She is researching her 'system's influence' for her PhD at the University of Bath and I am focusing on a draft abstract of her thesis.

Video 1 – First supervision session with Jacqueline Delong.
https://www.youtube.com/watch?v=4R1ilkWB9Dc.

There are numerous narratives I could construct using this video clip because there is an infinitude of knowledge in what I can be seen to be doing. The narrative I am going to tell is linked to the fundamental purpose of my research, which is to contribute to educational theories that can explain the influence of professional educators with their students and explain their influence on the education of social formations. In doing this I need to establish communicable standards of judgement for testing the validity of such explanations.

It may be helpful at this point to include the following assumption I bring into my educational relationships. Robyn Pound (1996), another practitioner-researcher I have worked alongside, transcribed a conversation with me and says that it was helpful in encouraging her to give credit to her own voice. It contains the meanings I seek to communicate to everyone I work with as I support their enquiries:

Here is an example of an affirming experience which encouraged me to give credit to my own voice. After a presentation I made during my first year, Jack Whitehead replied by saying:

At the moment the power behind what counts as knowledge is in the academy. It is not in the form of knowing that you have. I genuinely do believe that you have the form of knowledge that I am interested in helping to make public ... If we were to take the view that you are starting to work with parents of young children and that the knowing they have is developmental. It's emergent, but never-the-less is actually superior to the knowing that is in the academy at the moment about what you are interested in. You would have the personal and professional knowledge together (parents and me). We (the academy) would be the learners. Over a few years our task would be to learn what it is for you and your parents to become good parents with your help and support. We would be subordinate, in terms of our learning, to the personal and professional knowledge which you and the parents actually have as you are working with the child to become better parents. (Robyn Pound: taped presentation, Bath Action Research Group, 7.10.96).

One of the difficulties of communicating the meanings of embodied values in such educational relationships is connected to the limitation of words. Some meanings, especially those involving embodied values, often need non-verbal forms of expression as well as words to be experienced, understood and communicated (Hocking, Haskell and Linds, 2001). Hence the importance of JIME as a forum for sharing ideas that require multimedia forms of expression in the communication of meaning.

Communicating Meanings Of Embodied Values

As I have said, I am taking the context of the video to be my practice as a supervisor in which I am seeking to enable Jackie Delong, a practitioner-researcher, to submit a thesis that expresses her originality of mind and critical judgement. In Jackie's research these standards of judgement are related in an enquiry that includes an explanation of her 'system's influence' as a Superintendent of Schools. 'System's influence' is in Jackie's professional practice and research as a standard of judgement. This influence was recognised in an award for her leadership in Action Research by the Ontario Educational Research Council in December 2000.

A focus in what I am doing on the video is a draft abstract of her thesis. I am working to enhance the clarity of its communication of originality of mind and critical judgement in relation to 'system's influence'. I am also focusing on 'system's influence' because of a criticism made by Susan Noffke, about a limitation she perceived in the lack of capacity of theories generated from self-study to address:

> ... social issues in terms of the interconnections between personal identity and the claim of experiential knowledge, as well as power and privilege in society (Dolby, 1995; Noffke, 1991). The process of personal transformation through the examination of practice and self-reflection may be a necessary part of social change, especially in education; it is however, not sufficient (Noffke, 1997, p. 329).

By focusing on 'system's influence' in the context of social change I believe that the theories of practitioner-researchers can provide the evidence to show that Noffke is mistaken. I will address this point more fully in the fourth video clip below when I engage with the power relations within my own workplace. I will use this analysis to point to future possibilities for researching the education of social formations. I am thinking of research into a new scholarship of educational enquiry that engages with political, economic and cultural influences in the education of social formations.

In the second video clip below I give attention to the tension around the silence as I wait for Jackie's response to my criticism of the first draft of her abstract. My criticism was that I was unclear about the precise nature of her claims to originality of mind and critical judgement. Through my silence and in Jackie's response I claim that we can share meanings of my values and standards of originality of mind and critical judgement in relation to 'system's influence'.

In the third video clip I want to focus attention on the expression of pleasure (Foucault, p. 89, 1985) and humour (Bateson, p. 124, 1980) between us as we share our understandings of the 'improvements' in the second draft of her abstract. I also want to consider the possibility that pleasure and humour can be used as educational standards of judgement.

Finally I want to meet Noffke's criticism about power relations and privilege by moving onto an analysis of a fourth video clip that is focused on my engagement with the education of the social formation of the university. Here are the two drafts of the abstract produced within five days of each other. I have placed them together so that you may get a clearer understanding of the differences between them in the clarity with which they express the precise nature of the claims to originality of mind and critical judgement in relation to 'system's influence'. On reading the first draft I could not see clearly the precise nature of the claims to originality of mind and critical judgement.

First Draft of the Abstract

This thesis is a journey of professional learning, reinvention and self-discovery through research-based professionalism in asking the question, 'How do I improve my practice as a superintendent of schools in a southern Ontario school district?' It represents and demonstrates my originality of mind and critical judgement as I describe and explain my living standards of practice for which I hold myself accountable.

The values that I am articulating are grounded in my practice, in what I know from reading and dialogue, from experience and from reflecting on that experience. Through writing about my values that emerge in my practice, I am able to construct and deconstruct the transformation that has taken place over the six years of the research and to understand what has moved me forward.

Through narrative and image-based research I describe and explain the birth and growth of an action research movement in a school system that is restructuring amidst the negative pressures of market policies.

I offer my story as my own living-theory of my educative influence as an educational leader and insider researcher living in turbulent times – 1995–2001, not as a model or exemplar. I do, however, want to encourage professional educators to consider the process of practitioner action research as a means to self-assessment, renewal and professional development.

Second Draft of the Abstract

This thesis is my own living-theory of my learning about my educative influence as a superintendent of schools, an educational leader and insider researcher living in turbulent times – 1995–2001. It is a journey of professional learning and self-discovery through research-based professionalism as I ask, research and answer the question, 'How can I improve my practice as a superintendent of schools in a southern Ontario school district?'

It represents and demonstrates my originality of mind and critical judgement as I describe and explain my living standards of practice that can be understood through my values for which I hold myself accountable. My originality of mind is being expressed through narrative and image-based forms of communication in which I describe and explain stories of myself, a self-discovery of my need for internal and external dialogue, of how I hold together continuously in a living, dynamic way, a plurality of actions. I describe and explain my work in my many portfolios, including the birth and growth of an action research movement in a school system that is restructuring amidst the impact of economic rationalist policies.

This thesis focuses my critical judgements on the clarification and use of the values that have emerged in my practice as I am able to construct and deconstruct the transformations that have taken place over the six years of the research, and to understand what has moved me forward. The meaning of those values that I am articulating are grounded in my practice and constitute my living standards of practice and judgement in my explanations. They emerge through reading, dialogue and reflection on my experience as I account for myself in my practice by ever moving forward while holding onto the sanctity of personal relationships and democratic evaluation within a hierarchical system and power relations.

Here is the first video clip again, and a transcript of the conversation. I want to focus on the additional meanings which the visual record can communicate about the nature of our embodied values that we are using as our educational standards of practice and judgement.

Video clip 1 on 'systems influence'.

https://www.youtube.com/watch? v=4R1ilkWB9Dc.

Jack ... to show how I am encouraging and supporting you, to make explicit in a way that is publicly shareable your own understanding of your standard of practice as a superintendent which is related to your system's influence...

Jackie...there is a big emphasis on relationships and connections. That's a common standard that runs through almost everything I do – if I can see a way of helping people or ideas or systems to connect I think it creates a more effective system to support student learning. If you've got people or systems going in different directions it is wasting the talent and the energy... the other thing is that when I see people who can carry something forward I try to pull all the supports behind them so that they can do that. That's two pieces of it. It doesn't capture it all but it captures two pieces of – And my need to see things always getting better...

I want to focus both on the embodied values in Jackie's non-verbal expressions as well as her statements about her 'system's influence'.

I am thinking of the embodied values Jackie is expressing non-verbally when she is saying:

i.   If I can see a way of helping people or ideas or systems to connect I think it creates a more effective system to support student learning.

ii. When I see people who can carry something forward I try to pull all the supports behind them so that they can do that.

In her thesis Jackie writes about the importance for extending her system's influence of supporting people who she believes have the talent, energy and commitment to improve student learning. To understand what Jackie is meaning by her value of pulling all the supports behind them it is necessary to experience the sustained commitment she expresses over time in the organisation of this support. This in turn rests on her passion to improve learning with students.

All I want to do with video clip 1 is to make my point that multimedia forms of communication are significant for the definition and communication of the embodied values that help to constitute the unique individual 'I' of each of us in enquiries of the kind, 'How do I improve what I am doing?' I will now go on to justify my claim that they can also help to transform values into communicable standards of judgement.

To emphasise the importance of this process I think the following point from Jackie's second draft Abstract bears repeating:

This thesis focuses my critical judgements on the clarification and use of the values that have emerged in my practice as I am able to construct and deconstruct the transformations that have taken place over the six years of the research and to understand what has moved me forward. The meaning of those values that I am articulating are grounded in my practice and constitute my living standards of practice and judgement in my explanations. They emerge through reading, dialogue and reflection on my experience as I account for myself in my practice by ever moving forward while holding onto the sanctity of personal relationships and democratic evaluation within a hierarchical system and power relations.

In explaining my educational influence in relation to my values I want to be clear that I am not saying that I have educated my students. The only person I claim to have educated is myself. This distinction is important to me. I think that the influence of what I do, to be educative, must be mediated by the creativity and critical judgement of those who are learning with me. Because this is part of the way I understand education, I cannot claim to have educated someone else. I do, however, want to show below that my values are important in explanations of my influence in supporting student learning. I believe these explanations of my influence include my embodied values, as distinct from the values of others, in ways that are open to public tests of validity.

I now want to consider a second clip of a conversation with Jackie Delong. This shows her responding to my 'critical' judgements on the first draft abstract above. As I have said above in relation to the first abstract, I could not see clearly what she was defining in terms of her originality of mind and critical judgement. Do focus your attention on the non-verbal communications which you feel and see taking place. You may find it helpful to move the digital images rapidly backwards and forwards across the screen. Just be prepared for a period of silence at the beginning of the clip which marks Jackie's response to my 'critical' response to her first draft. As I wipe my brow I think you will vicariously experience my tension. Both of us live with the 'wait time' after my response. In my 'wait time' I am valuing and have faith in Jackie's capacity to exercise her originality of mind and critical judgement in responding to my concerns. After the silence, Jackie then moves on with an acknowledgement, through her acceptance of the criticism and exercise of her imagination, of what needs improving in her abstract. As the second draft shows (above) this explicitly refers to, and more clearly communicates, the nature of her originality of mind and critical judgement in her thesis.

Video 2 of supervision session in which Jacqueline Delong is responding to my own 'critical' response to her first abstract.

https://www.youtube.com/watch?v=w2kdOfRKFYs

I now want to draw your attention to two qualities I think I bring into my supervision. Researchers I have supervised tell me that these have had a positive influence on their learning. They tell me that I communicate a life-affirming pleasure in both their knowledge-creating capacities and faith in the embodied knowledge they already possess. Here is a video clip and still which show me expressing my pleasure with Jackie's second abstract, and Jackie expressing pleasure in my response in a way which carries, for both of us, this life-affirming energy. I don't want to ignore the significance of humour. The pleasure is accompanied by humour. Jackie had heard me complimenting another researcher on the wisdom of his practice and commenting that I hadn't used this term with her. I think you will experience the pleasure and humour at this point in the video clip. These qualities, when seen in relation to the tension involved in receiving and responding to criticism, we have agreed help to explain the sustaining and sustained relationships over the six-year period of the PhD research programme.

Video 3 of a supervision session at the end of a week working on the drafting and redrafting of the abstract for the PhD thesis.

https://www.youtube.com/watch?v=w2kdOfRKFYs.

I will now use multimedia to answer Noffke's (1997) criticism, that theories generated from self-studies do not seem capable of addressing issues of power and privilege in society. To answer this criticism I offer a self-study of my learning from experiences with a 1990 working party of the Senate of the University of Bath. This was established to investigate a claim from the Board of Studies of the School of Education that there was prima facie evidence of a breach of my academic freedom. This study is part of my research programme into the disciplinary foundations of a scholarship of educational enquiry (Whitehead, 1999, 2000b) and marks my move from solely text-based representations into multimedia.

The close connection to the first part of this paper, on values and living standards of judgement, is established through the idea of influencing the education of social formations through living values more fully in practice. If self-studies do not connect directly with the education of social formations then I believe Noffke's criticism stands.

I am approaching my self-study through Mitchell and Weber's (1999) notion of 'theorising nostalgia' and McIntyre and Cole's (2001) concept of a 'performance text'. The study includes an analysis of values of academic freedom, justice, power and privilege in the education of the social formation of my workplace. This education also includes my developing understanding of the influences of political economy in my workplace. The understanding develops as I engage with concepts of mythologising discourse, economic rationality, globalisation, communication, collective responsibility, collective intelligence and habitus in the work of Bernstein

(2000), Danaher (2001), McTaggart (1992), Habermas (1976, 1987), Whitty (1997), Brown and Lauder (2001) and Bourdieu (1990).

Mitchell and Weber (1999) recognise that the term 'nostalgia' can lead us into an arena laden with competing ideologies and perspectives. As they use it, nostalgia can be a liberating concept in the sense of a reinvention which uses what we know now to inform and critique what could have been. Much of what they explore involves a reclaiming of the past that acknowledges the fact that it is gone and can never be relived in the same way. Indeed, as they say, it may never have existed in exactly the way that we think it did. This does not mean that it is of no use, for memories can evoke a utopia towards which we can work. As they say, that's not how it was but how I would have wanted it to be, and how I want to make it for others:

> Reinvention through self-study can be a powerful and highly effective means of self-transformation and a catalyst for professional growth. It can strengthen or weaken hidden bits of self, challenging us to incorporate certain ignored elements into our professional identity, or forcing us to wrap our imagination around a different image of ourselves in action. It can be wonderfully motivating in its ability to bring home a painful or a beautiful truth, and help us appreciate and even bring about our most meaningful moments as teachers. Studying ourselves does not always involve major change; sometimes it is just about revaluing what was already there and using it in new ways that are informed by both the personal and the social (Mitchell and Weber, p. 232, 1999).

This is how I see myself revisiting and learning from the experiences of power relations in 1991 when I was invited to meet a Senate working party to discuss a matter of academic freedom (my own). It involves a combination of my nostalgic revisiting of my experience of the university working party with the idea of a performance text:

> Performance of the research text is an embodiment and representation of the inquiry process as well as a new process of active learning. The possibility of active learning in each performance or recreation of the text exists through our ongoing commitment to maintaining the conditions of our relationship. Each performance is an experiential basis for reflection, analysis, and learning because in relationship we are 'participants-as-collaborators' (Lincoln, 1993, p. 42). Together we were able to draw out each other's knowledge and strength. (McIntyre and Cole, p. 22, 2001).

Whenever I seek to make my own contribution to educational knowledge

(Whitehead, 1999, 2000b), I find myself remembering the history of the power relations and regimes of truth which have shaped the growth of my theory and knowledge. In the process of 'legitimating' my original ideas on the nature of educational theory and educational knowledge, I have been subjected to pressures which 'could have constrained a less determined individual'. These are not my words. They come from a report made to the Senate of the University of Bath in May 1991 by a working party established by Senate to investigate evidence concerning a matter of my academic freedom.

Earlier in this presentation I included video footage of my relationships with a practitioner-researcher which others have said shows something of the life-affirming energy and my passion for learning they experience with me. As I break with my traditional, text-based presentations in this submission to JIME, I now want to communicate the meanings of my response to the feelings of humiliation/defeat in the context of the Senate working party on a matter of academic freedom. I am thinking of a response which I characterise as the forceful assertion of scholarly values of freedom and justice. I am seeking to clarify the meanings of these values, in explanations for the education of the social formation of the university, in the course of their emergence from engagements with institutional power relations. In this way, I am seeking to answer Noffke's criticism by showing that it is possible for self-studies to engage with issues of power and privilege in the education of social formations.

I now ask you to accompany me into a performance text of a meeting with the four university colleagues who formed, in 1991, the Senate working party to investigate a matter of academic freedom in relation to my own work. The context was that the Board of Studies for Education had passed by one vote a recommendation to Senate that such an investigation should be carried out on the grounds that there was prima facie evidence that my academic freedom had been breached.

A preliminary report had been produced which concluded that my academic freedom had not been breached. There was no mention in the draft report that I had been subjected to any pressure. Here is a videotaped reconstruction, with a transcript of the 56-second clip of my 'reliving' of my passionate response to this preliminary report. The clip, made in 2001, begins at the point where I am finishing a description of the context of my meeting with the Senate working party, to a group of practitioner-researchers that meets weekly in the Department of Education:

Video 4 Reconstruction of my response to the working party on academic freedom. https://www.youtube.com/watch?v=MBTLfyjkFh0

Transcript:

I turned to walk from the room and here I paused and then I turned and I said:

> If you allow that report to be made public you are denying some of the fundamental values of what it means to be a scholar and an academic. If you don't recognise the pressure to which I've been subjected to in this institution since I came here in relation to my research, you are opening the doors for other abuses in relation to this institution. Now, that is all I have got to say to you, but if you permit that report to go to Senate in that form you are denying the fundamental responsibilities of being an academic.

Right,

and then I went.

My meeting with the committee to discuss the draft was followed by an inclusion in the final report which referred to pressure:

> The Working Party did not find that, in any of Mr. Whitehead's seven instances, his academic freedom had actually been breached. This was, however, because of Mr. Whitehead's persistence in the face of pressure; a less determined individual might well have been discouraged and therefore constrained.

This report was 'received' by Senate in May 1991.

At this point in my multimedia presentation I am drawing attention to the value of a visual medium and of 'theorising nostalgia' in understanding the education of social formations in facing the power relations that support the truth of power and the power of truth. For me, the education of social formations involves learning what it means for individuals to live their values in relation to the social formation more fully. It also means learning more about how to modify or transform the existing formation in order to support these living values more fully. By engaging with such power relations I think it is possible to meet Noffke's criticism and to show how living theories can engage with issues of power and privilege in society.

The power relations I have in mind are those which Foucault (1980, p. 133) describes in terms of regimes of truth. He writes about the regimes of truth in terms of the power relations which influence the procedures which determine what counts as truth in specific contexts. The contexts I have in mind are the Western academies within which power relations work to give higher status to propositional theories of professional knowledge, over the theories of practitioner-researchers generated from their self-studies. As an important aside, in relation to the education of the social formation of my University, I will mention that until 1991 research students were not permitted to question the competence of their examiners 'under any circumstances' once they had been appointed by Senate. In 1991 the regulation was changed to permit questions to be raised on the grounds of bias, prejudice and inadequate assessment. These are the kind of changes I am referring to when I write about the influence of self-studies in educating social formations.

Following Lomax (1997) I now want to take account of the way my enquiries engage in both an intersubjective and intrasubjective dialectic. When she writes about representing Action Research she means more than finding a new way of presenting data. By 'form of representation' she means a dynamic way of presenting the meaning of one's research that has two components: an intersubjective dialectic and an intrasubjective dialectic. She defines the intrasubjective dialectic as the process through which one's understanding is transformed as one engages in the struggle to represent what one means. This is the process I have been engaged in above. She defines the intersubjective dialectic as an engagement with the imagined or actual responses of others where the very act of representing is an invitation to others to engage. Lomax uses the word dialectic, because its implied 'openness' to learning is accompanied by purposeful self-knowledge that encourages argument rather than capitulation (Lomax, 1997).

In meeting Noffke's criticism I think it is important to show such an intersubjective engagement with the contributions of social theorists as I seek to enhance my understanding of the influence of my self-study on the education of a social formation. In particular I want to explain how I am seeking to avoid the kind of mythologising discourse described by Bernstein (2000) by which he claims schools disconnect the hierarchy of success internal to the school from social class hierarchies external to the school. He says that this involves the trick of creating a mythological discourse, and that this mythological discourse incorporates some of the political ideology and arrangement of the society:

> First of all, it is clear that conflict, or potential conflict, between social groups may be reduced or contained by creating a discourse which emphasises what all groups share, their communality, their apparent interdependence.

> By creating a fundamental identity, a discourse is created which generates what I shall call horizontal solidarities among their staff and students, irrespective of the political ideology and social arrangement of the society. The discourse which produces horizontal solidarities or attempts to produce such solidarities from this

point of view I call a mythological discourse. This mythological discourse consists of two pairs of elements which, although having different functions, combine to reinforce each other. One pair celebrates and attempts to produce a united, integrated, apparently common national consciousness; the other pair work together to disconnect hierarchies within the school from a causal relation with social hierarchies outside the school (p. xxiii).

What I am seeking to do is to show that my developing understanding of political economy in my self-study of my influence on the education of social formations can engage with issues of power and privilege in society. I am thinking of forms of engagement that avoid the creation of a mythologising discourses while contributing to the education of social formations. I believe that the following ideas on globalisation, economic rationality, communication, decision-making and collective intelligence are helping to develop these forms of engagement. Danaher (2001) has articulated two varieties of globalisation in a way that clarifies my own understandings:

There are really two varieties of globalisation: élite globalisation and grassroots globalisation. The top-down globalisation is characterised by a constant drive to maximise profits for globe-spanning corporations. It forces countries to 'open up' their national economies to large corporations, reduce social services, privatise state functions, deregulate the economy, be 'efficient' and competitive, and submit everything and everyone to the rule of 'market forces'. Because markets move resources only in the direction of those with money, social inequality has reached grotesque levels. But there is another kind of globalisation that centres on life values: protecting human rights and the environment. Grassroots globalisation comprises many large and growing movements: the fair trade movement, micro-enterprise lending networks, the movement for social and ecological labelling, sister cities and sister schools, citizen diplomacy, trade union solidarity across borders, worker owned co-ops, international family farm networks, and many others (Danaher, p. 25, 2001).

McTaggart (1992) explains how economic rationalism can lead to devaluation and demoralisation:

Economic rationalism is not merely a term which suggests the primacy of economic values. It expresses commitment to those values in order to serve particular sets of interests ahead of others. Furthermore, it disguises that commitment in a discourse of 'economic necessity' defined by its economic models. We have moved beyond the reductionism which leads all questions to be discussed as if they were economic ones (de-valuation) to a situation where moral questions are denied completely (de-moralisation) in a cult of economic inevitability (as if greed had nothing to do with it) (McTaggart, p. 50, 1992).

From Habermas (1977) I use ideas on the validity claims we make in reaching mutual understanding and, I would add, to avoid mythologising discourses. That is, our communications should be comprehensible. We should provide evidence for our assertions. We should reveal the normative background of our communication and we should reveal our authenticity in interaction through time.

From Habermas' (1987) view of the tasks of a critical theory I use the following point about the importance of focusing on learning at a given time:

A theory developed in this way can no longer start by examining concrete ideals immanent in traditional forms of life. It must orient itself to the range of learning processes that is opened up at a given time by a historically attained level of learning. It must refrain from critically evaluating and normatively ordering totalities, forms of life and cultures, and life-contexts and epochs as a whole (Habermas, p. 383, 1987).

I also identify with Whitty's (1997) analysis of quasi-markets in education with his call for collective responsibility:

Part of the challenge must be to move away from atomized decision making to the reassertion of collective responsibility without re-creating the very bureaucratic systems whose shortcomings have helped to legitimate the current tendency to treat education as a private good rather than a public responsibility (p. 37).

Where I differ from Whitty is in the belief that it is important not to move away from atomised decision-making but to deepen and extend this decision-making in the reassertion of collective responsibility. I am thinking of deepening an appreciation of individual decision-making and responsibility in relation to one's own values, while at the same time working to strengthen forums for the development of collective responsibility.

I see the exercise of both individual and collective responsibility as being intimately linked to Brown and Lauder's (2001) call for the development of collective intelligence:

Collective intelligence can be defined as empowerment through the development and pooling of intelligence to attain common goals or resolve common problems .... the struggle for collective intelligence therefore involves more than a democratization of intelligence, it involves making a virtue of our mutual dependence and sociability which we will need to make a dominant feature of post-industrial society based on information, knowledge and lifelong learning (pp. 218–219).

In developing educational theories that include collective intelligence in explaining the education of social formations I am wondering about the validity of the claim that 'No sophisticated theory of education can ignore its contribution to economic development' (Halsey, Lauder, Brown and Wells, 1997, p. 156).

The theories in the Living Theory section of http://www.actionresearch. net acknowledge the influence of economic forces without engaging with their contribution to economic development. My present position is that it is possible to create sophisticated and valid theories of education that acknowledge the influence of economic development without engaging with the contribution of education or educational theory to that development. I also want to respond with the additional claim that no sophisticated theory of education can ignore the embodied knowledge in educational practice. In making this point I want to stress that I see fundamental differences in the logic and language between the 'outsider' researcher's theories and those of 'insider' self-study researchers. I am making a distinction between philosophical, sociological, psychological, historical, economic, political and management theories, and educational theories that can explain the educational influence of educators with their students and can explain the education of social formations. I am thinking of the contributions to educational theory being made by professional educators as they engage in disciplined forms of self-study of their own professional learning (Hamilton and Pinnegar, 1998; Ghaye and Ghaye, 1998; McNiff, 2000b).

Working with Bourdieu's (1990) ideas, I live with the following tension between an insider practitioner-researcher, who integrates insights from 'outsider' social theorists into his 'insider' living theorising of the education of social formations:

An agent who possesses a practical mastery, an art, whatever it may be, is capable of applying in his action the disposition which appears to him only in action, in the relationship with a situation (he can repeat the feint which strikes him as the only thing to do, as often as the situation requires). But he is no better placed to perceive what really governs his practice and to bring it to the order of discourse, than the observer, who has the advantage over him of being able to see the action from outside, as an object, and especially of being able to totalize the successive realizations of the habitus (without necessarily having the practical mastery that underlies these realizations or the adequate theory of this mastery). And there is every reason to think that as soon as he reflects on his practice, adopting a quasi-theoretical posture, the agent loses any chance of expressing the truth of his practice, and especially the truth of the practical relation to the practice (Bourdieu, pp. 90–91, 1992).

When I see this word 'totalize' used in the context of theory generation I pay attention to Habermas' point above, about avoiding such a tendency and about the importance of focusing on a range of learning processes.

Finally, I pay attention to Bourdieu's insights that a conformity to objective demands, through the habitus has nothing to do with rules and conscious compliance with rules. On this point Bourdieu is critical of social science theories in analysing social formations:

> The objective adjustment between dispositions and structures ensures a conformity to objective demands and urgencies which has nothing to do with rules and conscious compliance with rules, and gives an appearance of finality which in no way implies conscious positing of the ends objectively attained. Thus, paradoxically, social science makes greatest use of the language of rules precisely in the cases where it is most totally inadequate, that is, in analysing social formations in which, because of the constancy of the objective conditions over time, rules have a particularly small part to play in the determination of practices, which is largely entrusted to the automatisms of the habitus. (Bourdieu, p. 145, 1990).

In seeking to show how self-studies of educational practice can engage with issues of power and privilege in society I am aware of the danger of creating a mythologising discourse. I am thinking of a discourse about the education of social formations that simply serves the existing habitus in reproducing the formations, rather than contributing to their transformation.

I am now at the limit of my present understanding in accounting for the way in which power relations in the regime of truth in the university have influenced the legitimation of educational theories and have themselves been influenced by relations of political economy. For readers interested in testing my claim that educational theories with their living standards of judgement have been 'legitimated' in the academy, the titles, PhD and master's enquiries in the Living Theory section of

http://www.actionresearch.net

may repay your attention:

Austin, T. (2001) *Treasures In The Snow: What Do I Know And How Do I Know It Through My Educational Inquiry Into My Practice Of Community?* PhD thesis, University of Bath, In the Living Theory section of http://www.actionresearch.net/

Adler-Collins, J. (2000) *A Scholarship Of Enquiry,* MA dissertation, University of Bath. In the Living Theory section of http://www.actionresearch.net.

Cunningham, B. (1999) *How Do I Come To Know My Spirituality As I Create My Own Living-Educational-Theory?* PhD thesis, University of Bath. In the Living Theory section of http://www.actionresearch.net.

D'Arcy, P. (1998) *The Whole Story...* PhD thesis, University of Bath. In the Living Theory section of http://www.actionresearch.net.

Eames, K. (1995) *How Do I, As A Teacher And Educational Action-Researcher, Describe And Explain The Nature Of My Professional Knowledge?* PhD thesis, University of Bath. In the Living Theory section of http://www.actionresearch.net.

Finnegan (2000) *How Do I Create My Own Educational Theory As An Action Researcher And As A Teacher?* PhD thesis University of Bath. In the Living Theory section of http://www.actionresearch.net.

Holley, E. (1997) *How Do I As A Teacher-Researcher Contribute To The Development Of A Living-Educational-Theory Through An Exploration Of My Values In My Professional Practice?* M.Phil., University of Bath. In the Living Theory section of http://www.actionresearch.net.

Hughes, J. (1996) *Action Planning And Assessment In Guidance Contexts: How Can I Understand And Support These Processes While Working With Colleagues In Further Education Colleges And Career Service Provision In Avon.* PhD thesis, University of Bath. In the Living Theory section of http://www.actionresearch.net.

Laidlaw, M. (1996) *How Can I Create My Own Living-Educational-Theory As I Offer You An Account Of My Educational Development?* PhD thesis, University of Bath. In the Living Theory section of http://www.actionresearch.net.

Loftus, J. (1999) *An Action Enquiry Into The Marketing Of An Established First School In Its Transition To Full Primary Status.* PhD thesis, Kingston University. In the Living Theory section of http://www.actionresearch.net.

Evans, M. (1995) *An Action Research Enquiry Into Reflection In Action As Part Of My Role As A Deputy Head Teacher.* PhD thesis, Kingston University. In the Living Theory section of http://www.actionresearch.net .

Whitehead, J. (1999) *How Do I Improve My Practice? Creating A Discipline Of Education Through Educational Enquiry.* PhD thesis, University of Bath. In the Living Theory section of http://www.actionresearch.net.

This paper is based on the assumption that the expression, definition and communication of living standards of practice and judgement, through multimedia communications, could hold the key to the development of a new epistemology in the new scholarship of educational enquiry (Schön, 1995). I am thinking of an epistemology that integrates the life-values of individuals and groups into the living standards of practice and judgement they use in both creating themselves, their social formations and their educational knowledge.

I have argued that a serious limitation of text-based presentations is that the meanings of embodied values and their inclusion in explanations of educative influence tend to be eliminated in propositional forms of communication. JIME offers a forum that enables a critical and creative engagement with the visual records and explanations of what practitioner-researchers are doing in their own educational enquiries of the kind, 'How can I help you to improve your learning?' and 'How can we enhance our influence in the education of social formations?' This multimedia forum offers a unique opportunity to reconstruct educational theory through the expression, definition and communication of a values-based approach to living standards of judgement. It also offers a public forum for testing claims to educational knowledge that can relate practitioner-research to both the education of individuals and the education of social formations.

Bibliography

Bateson, G. (1980) *Mind and Nature*. p. 124. New York: Bantam.

Bernstein, B. (2000) *Pedagogy, Symbolic Control and Identity: Theory, Research, Critique*. Lanham, Boulder, New York, Oxford: Rowman & Littlefield.

Bourdieu, P. (1990) *The Logic of Practice*. Cambridge: Blackwell.

Brown, P. and Lauder, H. (2001) *Capitalism and Social Progress*. Basingstoke: Palgrave.

Burke, A. (1992) *Teaching: Retrospect and Prospect*. Footnote 6 on p. 222, OIDEAS, Vol. 39, pp. 5–254.

Danaher, K. (2001) *Power to the People*, p. 25, London: The Observer.

Eisner, E. (1993) Forms of Understanding and the Future of Educational Research. *Educational Researcher*, 22(7); 5–11.

Foucault, M. (1980) Truth and Power, in *Power/Knowledge*, Gordon, C. (Ed.) (1980). Brighton: Harvester.

Foucault, M. (1985) *The Use of Pleasure*, London: Penguin.

Ghaye, A. and Ghaye, K. (1998) *Teaching and Learning through Critical Reflective Practice*. London: David Fulton.

Habermas, J. (1976) *Legitimation Crisis*. London: Heinemann.

Habermas, J. (1987) *Theory of Communicative Action, Vol. 2*. Cambridge: Polity.

Halsey, A.H. (Ed.) (1997) *Education: culture, economy and society*. Oxford: Oxford University Press.

Hamilton, M.L. and Pinnegar, S. (1998) Conclusion, in Hamilton, M.L. (Ed.) (1998) *Reconceptualising Teaching Practice: self-study in teacher education*. London: Falmer.

Hocking, B., Haskell, J. and Linds, W. (Eds.) (2001) *Unfolding Bodymind: Exploring Possibility Through Education*. Brandon, VT: Psychology Press/Holistic Education Press.

Husserl, E. (1931) *Ideas: General Introduction to Pure Phenomenology*. London: George Allen & Unwin.

Laidlaw, M. (1996) *How Can I Create My Own Living-Educational-Theory As I Offer You An Account Of My Educational Development?* PhD thesis, University of Bath. In the Living Theory Section of http://www.actionresearch.net.

Lather, P. (2000) *Paradigm Talk Revisited: How else might we characterise the proliferation of research perspectives within our field?* Paper to AERA, New Orleans, April 2000.

Lomax, P. (1997) *Sharing an agenda for the future: issues and debates in action research*. Keynote to the 1997 Collaborative Action Research Network Annual Conference on Collaborative Action Research Through The Spectrum.

McIntyre, M. and Cole, A.L. (2001) Conversations in Relation: the research relationship in/as artful self-study. *Reflective Practice*, 2(1); 526.

McNiff, J. (2000a) (Ed.) *Educational Research in Ireland*. Dublin: September Books.

McNiff, J. (2000b) *Action Research in Organisations*. London; New York: Routledge.

McTaggart, R. (1992) Reductionism and Action Research: Technology versus convivial forms of life, in Bruce, S. and Russell, A.L. *Transforming Tomorrow Today*. Published by Action Learning, Action Research and Process Management Association Incorporated, Brisbane, Australia, 1992.

Mills, G. (2000) *Action Research: A guide for the teacher researcher*. New Jersey, Columbus: Merrill, Prentice Hall.

Mitchell, C. and Weber, S. (1999) *Reinventing Ourselves as Teachers: Beyond Nostalgia*. London: Falmer.

Noffke, S. (1997) Professional, Personal, and Political Dimensions of Action Research in, Apple, M. (Ed.) (1997) *Review of Research in Education*, Vol. 22, Washington: AERA.

Pound, R. (1996) Transcript of taped conversation with J. Whitehead. Bath University Action Research Group.

Schön, D. (1995) The need for a new epistemology for the new scholarship. *Change*, November/December.

Snow, C.E. (2001) Knowing What We Know: Children, Teachers, Researchers. Presidential Address to AERA, 2001, in Seattle, in *Educational Researcher*, 30(7); 3–9.

Whitehead, J. (1999) *How do I improve my practice? Creating a discipline of education through educational enquiry*. PhD thesis, University of Bath, in the Living Theory section of http://www.actionresearch.net.

Whitehead, J. (2000a) How do I improve my practice? Creating and legitimating an epistemology of practice. *Reflective Practice*, Vol. 1, No. 1, pp. 91–104.

Whitehead, J. (2000b) *Living standards of research, reflection and renewal*. Keynote address presented at the conference of the Ontario Educational Research Council. December 2000.

Whitty, G. (1997) Creating Quasi-Markets in Education, in Apple, M. (1997) (Ed.) *Review of Research in Education*, Washington: AERA.

Zeichner, K. (1999) The new scholarship in teacher education. *Educational Researcher*, 28; 4–15. The original ideas in this paper were presented at AERA, Seattle, Session, Division D3, Session 44.09, Alternative Paradigms, Methods and Analysis in Qualitative Research in Education, 14 April 2001.

PAPER FOUR.

Whitehead, J. (2008) Using A Living-Theory Methodology in Improving Practice and Generating *Educational Knowledge in Living Theories. EJOLTS*, 1(1); 103–126.

http://ejolts.net/node/80.

This paper focuses attention on the importance of recognising that in the generation of a living-educational-theory an individual is evolving their own living-theory methodology. The evolution of the methodology occurs in the course of its emergence in the process of the enquiry. This is not the same as 'applying' a pre-existing methodology to the enquiry. A living-educational-theory can integrate insights from different methodologies, such as Autoethnography, Action Research, Narrative Enquiry and Phenomenology, into the generation of a living-theory methodology without this methodology being subsumed under any existing methodology. Because of the earlier, very significant influence of Action Research in my educational enquiry, I want to emphasise that the originality of the idea of a living-educational-theory cannot be subsumed within an Action Research paradigm. However, I also want to stress that I continue to use insights from Action Research, such as the action-reflection cycles, within the generation of my living-educational-theory.

I make a clear distinction between the methods I use in my enquiries and the methodology I generate in the creation of a living-educational-theory. By methodology I mean the principles that explain how I carried out my research. By methods, I mean the tools I use to gather data, such as the use of an action-reflection cycle, or to subject my analysis to the mutual rational control of critical discussion with the use of a validation group.

In explaining educational influences in learning, the paper also explicates the epistemologies that distinguish Living Theories using the ideas of the unit of appraisal, living standards of judgement and living logics. The unit is the individual's explanation of their educational influence in learning. The standards of judgement are the values and understandings the researcher uses to explain their educational influences in learning and that can be used to evaluate the validity of the researcher's claim to be making a contribution to educational knowledge. The living logic is the mode of thought in a living-educational-theory that distinguishes the theory as rational (Marcuse, 1964, p. 105). Epistemology is the focus of Paper Four. This was presented in the keynote symposium of the 2009

British Educational Research Association on 'Explicating A New Epistemology For Educational Knowledge With Educational Responsibility'.

Using digital visual data from my educational practice, the paper explicates and communicates the explanatory principles and standards of judgement that are needed in recognising this educational researcher as a knowledge-creator. The idea of educational influences in learning is meant to provide a different understanding of educational relationships to those researchers that use the idea of causal relationships in explaining educational influences in learning. Educational influences in learning from a Living Theory perspective are grounded in the idea that the relationships between educator and students are intentional, rather than causal relations. Whatever the educator does is mediated by the learner responses to what the educator is doing. This mediation involves some degree of conscious awareness of the learner for the learning to be recognised as educational in Living Theory research. In recognising what is 'educational' I explain in the paper why I believe that it is necessary to make a clear distinction between education research and educational research.

The paper also provides evidence to show the moment, in a keynote presentation to the International Conference of Teacher Research in New York, that I can rechannel the anger I express, in remembering the conflicts described in Paper Two, in responding to attempts to terminate my employment. The rechannelling shows my expression of the anger, that I recognise could have become pathological and damaging, into the life-affirming energy and love for what I am doing, as explanatory principles in explanations of educational influences in my own learning.

PAPER FOUR.

Using a Living-Theory Methodology in Improving Practice and Generating Educational Knowledge in Living-Theories.

Abstract

The approach outlined below is focused on a living-theory methodology for improving practice and generating knowledge from questions of the kind 'How do I improve what I am doing?' It also includes a new epistemology for educational knowledge. The new epistemology rests on a living logic of educational enquiry and living standards of judgement (Laidlaw, 1996) that include flows of life-affirming energy with values that carry hope for the future of humanity.

The presentation emphasises the importance of the uniqueness of each individual's living-educational-theory (Whitehead, 1989) in improving practice and generating knowledge. It emphasises the importance of individual creativity in contributing to improving practice and knowledge from within historical and cultural opportunities and constraints in the social contexts of the individual's life and work.

The web-based version of this presentation demonstrates the importance of local, national and international communicative collaborations for improving practice and generating knowledge in the context of globalising communications. Through its multimedia representations of educational relationships and explanations of educational influence in learning it seeks to communicate new living standards of judgement. These standards are relationally dynamic and grounded in both improving practice and generating knowledge. They express the life-affirming energy of individuals, cultures and the cosmos, with values and understandings that it is claimed carry hope for the future of humanity.

a) What Is A Living-Theory?

A living-theory is an explanation produced by an individual for their educational influence in their own learning, in the learning of others, and in the learning of the social formation in which they live and work.

i) Why did I feel the need for a living-theory?

In 1967, in my special study on my initial teacher education programme, A Way To Professionalism In Education, I wrote about the importance of a professional knowledge base for education. In my later studies of educational theory between 1968 and 1972 I began to see that the dominant view of educational theory, known as the disciplines approach, was mistaken. It was known as the disciplines approach because it was constituted by the disciplines of philosophy, psychology, sociology and history of education.

The mistake was in thinking that disciplines of education could explain the educational influences of individuals in their own and in each other's learning. The error was not grounded in mistakes in the disciplines of education. The mistake was in the disciplines approach to educational theory. The mistake was in thinking that the disciplines of education, individually or in any combination, could explain adequately an individual's educational influence in their own learning and in the learning of others.

My recognition of this mistake between 1971 and 1972 came midway through my studies for a master's degree in the psychology of education. As I was conducting a controlled experiment design for my dissertation on the way adolescents acquired scientific understanding, I began to feel a tension between an explanation that assumed individual learners could be validly represented in dependent and independent variables and an explanation I constructed for my educational influence that was grounded in my conscious lived experience. I also began to see that my explanations for my educational influences in the learning of my pupils could not be subsumed within any conceptual framework in the psychology of education or any existing discipline of education. This recognition refocused my vocation. It moved from being a schoolteacher, teaching pupils science in secondary schools, to becoming a university academic and educational researcher, researching the creation and academic legitimation of valid forms of educational theory. Such theories could explain the educational influences of individuals in their own learning and in the learning of others. I believed then and still believe now that the profession of education requires such a professional knowledge base.

My move to the University of Bath in 1973 was motivated by this desire to contribute to the creation and legitimation of educational theory. I continue to identify with the mission of the University of Bath, which includes having a distinct academic approach to the education of professional practitioners.

The damage inflicted on the teaching profession by the disciplines approach to educational theory may be judged from the fact that Hirst, a main proponent, acknowledged a mistake in the following two quotations from 1983, where he says that much understanding of educational theory will be developed:

> ... in the context of immediate practical experience and will be co-terminous with everyday understanding. In particular, many of its operational principles, both explicit and implicit, will be of their nature generalisations from practical

experience and have as their justification the results of individual activities and practices. (Hirst, 1983, p. 18).

The damage can be appreciated through Hirst's understanding that the practical principles you and I use to explain our educational influences in our own learning and in the learning of others would be replaced by principles with more theoretical justification:

> In many characterisations of educational theory, my own included, principles justified in this way have until recently been regarded as at best pragmatic maxims having a first crude and superficial justification in practice that in any rationally developed theory would be replaced by principles with more fundamental, theoretical justification. That now seems to me to be a mistake. Rationally defensible practical principles, I suggest, must of their nature stand up to such practical tests and without that are necessarily inadequate. (ibid.)

The hegemony of the disciplines of education continues to dominate what counts as educational research. As Allender and Allender (2008) point out:

> The belief that educational research trumps practice, historically and still, is one of the major obstacles. The results of scholarly enquiry have managed to become the top of a top-down world. The not-so-subtle message is that there is a better known way to teach and teachers ought to change their practices accordingly. And, teachers have a way of willingly participating in this system when they persist in searching for the new trick to quickly and magically make their teaching easier. Progress depends on giving up the hegemony of scholarly enquiry. Knowledge has many sources, and they are best honored when they are used as part of a lively dialectic. The obvious shift is for teachers to give themselves credit for having an expertise that is uniquely valuable to themselves, and others. (pp. 127–128).

Allender and Allender also believe that:

> somewhere in history, the status of the teaching profession lost ground – setting up teachers to be viewed as incompetent. They believe that this view handicaps every teacher, and that there is a dire need to escape this undeserved status (ibid., p. 128).

It may be that, by clearly distinguishing what counts as education research from educational research, in terms of new living standards of judgement, valid forms of educational knowledge and educational theory could be legitimated in the Academy.

ii) Making a clear distinction between education research and educational research

I am suggesting that education research is research carried out from the perspectives of disciplines and fields of education such as the philosophy, sociology, history, psychology, management, economics, policy and leadership of education. In my view, educational research is distinguished as the creation and legitimation of valid forms of educational theory and knowledge that can explain the educational influences of individuals in their own learning, in the learning of others and in the learning of the social formations in which we live and work.

This focus on the epistemological significance of what counts as educational knowledge has been highlighted by Bruce Ferguson (2008) where she notes that the increase in diverse perspectives and presentation styles in research is indicative of an epistemological transformation in what counts as educational knowledge (p. 24).

Stimulated to respond to Bruce Ferguson's point I claim that this epistemological transformation will require new forms of representation and educational standards of judgement in journals of educational research (Whitehead, 2008a). In this contribution to *EJOLTS* I am directing attention to how the evidence, showing the nature of these forms of representation and living standards of judgement, can be accessed by those with the technology to do so. The evidence includes multimedia representations of flows of energy and values in the embodied knowledge of educators and their students. I recognise that the development of such representations costs money. Access to the most advanced technology of the day, with the use of the communicative power of the internet, has economic implications.

My own research programme has benefited from access to this technology. I also acknowledge the influence of the economic context on my research programme in that I have held a tenured contract at the University of Bath with secure employment from 1973 to the end of the contract in 2009. I do not want to underestimate the importance of this economic security in my capacity to keep open a creative space at the University to develop my research programme.

In making a clear distinction between education and educational research and acknowledging the importance of technology and economics, I also want it to be understood that I value the integration of insights from the theories from education researchers into my own living theories. For example, the historical and cultural contexts of my workplace are Western and mainly white. These contexts are changing with multicultural and postcolonial influences (Charles, 2007; Murray, 2007) questioning the power relations that sustain unjust privileges and the dominant logic and languages that sustain what counts as knowledge in the Western academies.

In my early work between 1967 and 1973 I followed this dominant logic and language. By this I mean that I used a positivist and propositional view of knowledge derived from the influence of my first degree in physical science. In my positivist phase I believed that controlled experimental designs gave access to the highest form of knowledge and that the theories generated from this approach should be presented within propositional statements about sets of variables that excluded contradictions. During the middle period of my research between 1977 and 1999 I extended my epistemological understandings to include dialectics (Ilyenkov, 1977) with its nucleus of contradiction. Since 2003 I have been exploring the implications of an epistemology of inclusionality (Rayner, 2004) which has much in common with African, Eastern and other indigenous ways of knowing (Bruce Ferguson, 2008). I want to stress again that this is not to imply a rejection of all my insights from propositional and dialectical theories. I continue to value insights from these theories as I deepen and extend my understandings of living-educational-theories and a living-theory methodology with the evolution of the implications of asking, researching and answering 'How do I improve what I am doing?'

I will examine below the significance of these epistemological understandings of propositions, dialectics and inclusionality when I consider the use of a living-theory methodology in the processes of improving practice and in the generation of educational knowledge. In this process I follow Ryle's insight:

[e]fficient practice precedes the theory of it; methodologies presuppose the application of the methods, of the critical investigation of which they are the products. (Ryle, 1973, p. 31).

b) What Is A Living-Theory Methodology?

i) Using action-reflection cycles as a method

My understanding of action-reflection cycles emerged from my practical question, 'How do I improve what I am doing?' The method emerged before my awareness of its significance as a research question. I asked this question on my first day in 1967 as a science teacher in Langdon Park School, a London comprehensive school. I felt a passion to help my students to improve their scientific understandings. In my first lessons I could see that my pupils were not comprehending much of what I was saying and doing. However, I did not feel my concern to be grounded in a 'deficit' model of myself. I felt a confidence that, while what was going on was not as good as it could be, I would be able to contribute to improvements. My imagination worked to offer possibilities about improving what I was doing. I chose a possibility to act on, and acted and evaluated the effectiveness of what

I was doing in terms of my communications with my pupils. This disciplined process of problem forming and solving is what I call an action reflection method.

ii) Developing an understanding of a living-theory methodology

A methodology is not only a collection of the methods used in the research. It is distinguished by a philosophical understanding of the principles that organise the 'how' of the enquiry. A living-theory methodology explains how the enquiry was carried out in the generation of a living-theory.

For example, my awareness of the importance of improving practice is grounded in my passion to see values of freedom, justice, compassion, respect for persons, love and democracy lived as fully as possible. Hence, in my living-theory methodology, you should expect to see the meanings of these values emerge in the course of my practice. Because the expression of energy in the meanings of these values cannot be communicated using only words on pages of text, I will use video data in a visual narrative to help with the public communication of these meanings.

One of the distinguishing characteristics of Action Research from action learning is that the researcher must make public the story of their research in a way that is open to others to evaluate its validity. A living-theory methodology includes the processes of validation.

I work with Polanyi's (1958) decision about personal knowledge. This is a decision to understand the world from my own point of view as an individual claiming originality and exercising judgement responsibly with universal intent. I know that the local identity of my 'I' is influenced by the non-local flows of space and energy through the cosmos. Yet I do work with a sense of responsibility for the educational influences I have in my own learning. I also recognise myself as a unique human being with this responsibility and I do exercise a sense of personal responsibility in validating for myself my claims for what I believe to be true. In doing this I take account of responses from a process of social validation I have developed from the ideas of Macdonald and Habermas.

Since 1976 I have used a process of democratic evaluation, described by Macdonald (1976), together with the four criteria of social validity proposed by Habermas (1976), to strengthen the personal and social validity of living theories. By this I mean that I submit my explanations of educational influence to a validation group of peers with a request that they help me to strengthen the comprehensibility, truthfulness, rightness and authenticity of the explanation. Within comprehensibility I include the logic of the explanation as a mode of thought that is appropriate for comprehending the real as rational (Marcuse, 1964, p. 105). Within truthfulness I include the evidence for justifying the assertions I make in my claims to knowledge. Within rightness I include an awareness of the normative assumptions I am making in the values that inform my claims to knowledge. Within authenticity I include the evidence of interaction over time that I am truly committed to living the values I explicitly espouse.

The social sciences have influenced what counts as educational research. Some researchers believe that educational research is distinguishable as a social science. I do not share this belief. My reasons are related to my meanings of educational and social where my meanings of educational cannot be subsumed within my meanings of social. Here are my meanings of social and educational to explain my understandings of some differences.

My meanings of 'social' in social validity, social action, social behaviour and social formations are influenced by the ideas of Habermas (1976) as described above, Schütz (1967) and Bourdieu (1990). I am most influenced in my meanings of social, social action and social behaviour by the work of Alfred Schütz in his *Phenomenology of the Social World*:

> Following the logic of our own terminology, we prefer to take as our starting point, not social action or social behavior, but intentional conscious experiences directed toward the other self. However, we include here only these intentional experiences which are related to the other as other, that is, as a conscious living being. We are leaving out of account intentional Acts directed only to the other person's body as a physical object rather than as a field of expression for his subjective experiences. Conscious experiences intentionally related to another self which emerge in the form of spontaneous activity we shall speak of as social behaviour. If such experiences have the character of being previously projected, we shall speak of them as social action (Schütz, 1967, p. 144).

What I take from this is that a social action can be distinguished from social behaviour by the spontaneous activity in behaviour and the previous projection in an action.

In using the idea of social formations in such phrases as the 'educational influences in the learning of social formations' I want to distinguish educational influences in one's own learning and in the learning of others from the educational influences in the learning of a social formation such as a university. Because of cultural and historical influences in the social contexts in which we live and learn I want to acknowledge the importance of having an educational influence in the learning of such social formations. I know that the nature of meaning is complex, but I think we can work with the idea of educational influences in the learning of social formations as being highly significant. For example, when the University of Bath changed the regulations governing its social formation in 2004 to allow the submission of e-media. I refer to this as an educational influence in the learning of a social formation. I think of it as an educational influence because it has extended the cognitive range and concerns of the forms of representation that can be used in the public communication of living-educational-theories.

I take the form of something to be fundamental in making sense of it. I need form to make sense. If something doesn't have a form I find that I cannot comprehend it. I use social formation in the sense used by Bourdieu in his point about the analysis of social formations in relation to the habitus:

> The objective adjustment between dispositions and structures ensures a conformity to objective demands and urgencies which has nothing to do with rules and conscious compliance with rules, and gives an appearance of finality which in no way implies conscious positing of the ends objectively attained. Thus, paradoxically, social science makes greatest use of the language of rules precisely in the cases where it is most totally inadequate, that is, in analysing social formations in which, because of the constancy of the objective conditions over time, rules have a particularly small part to play in the determination of practices, which is largely entrusted to the automatisms of the habitus (Bourdieu, 1990, p. 145).

I want to be clear that I do not subsume the experience and expression of the life-affirming energy in my explanations of educational influences in learning to meanings of 'social'. My educational relationships are social in the sense that they can be distinguished as intentional conscious experiences directed toward the other self (Schütz, 1967, p. 144). However, my explanations for my educational influences include the non-social flows of life-affirming energy that distinguish my social relations as educational.

Whilst expressing this life-affirming energy in my social relations I want to emphasise that I bring energy that flows from outside the social through the cosmos into my educational relationships. I use the expression of this energy in my accounts to distinguish what is educational from social relations. Hence, I do not subsume my understanding of what is educational to a concept of 'social' in the improvement of practice and in the generation of knowledge. At the same time I recognise the importance of social relations in influencing my educational relationships.

c) Improving Practice With A Living-Theory Methodology

i) The importance of forming good questions

I like the point made by Collingwood about the relationship between propositions and questions:

Whether a given proposition is true or false, significant or meaningless, depends on what question it was meant to answer; and any one who wishes to know whether a given proposition is true or false, significant or meaningless, must first find out what question it is was meant to answer (Collingwood, 1991, p. 39).

The questions we ask about our practice can be influential in what we do. For me, a good question for improving practice is: 'How do I improve what I am doing?' I found myself asking this question in the first lesson I taught in 1967. During this lesson I found myself feeling that I was not helping the pupils to improve their learning as well as I could. The question flowed with a life-affirming energy to do better. It flowed with the values and understandings of scientific enquiry and knowledge I brought into my work as a teacher of science.

Some 41 years after asking this question and asking, researching and answering it continuously in my research programme, I am still finding it a good question. It is at the heart of my focus on seeing what I can do to understand better how to enable the responses of educators to their pupils and students to be included in explanations of educational influence in learning. I am thinking of an educational influence that supports individuals to create their own living-educational-theories of their lives and learning as they seek to improve their practice.

ii) Using action-reflection cycles in improving practice

From the ground of a good question such as 'How do I improve what I am doing?' I found my imagination worked spontaneously in generating ideas about how I might improve my practice. I consciously chose one possibility to act on and formed an action plan. I acted and evaluated the effectiveness of my actions. In 1967 I followed this action-reflection cycle intuitively as I began my work in education and only made it explicit later (Whitehead, 1976).

Making it explicit helped me to see the importance of strengthening the data I collected to make a judgement on the effectiveness of my actions and understandings. Making it explicit also helped me to understand just how important it is, for the creation of valid explanations of educational influences in learning, to submit one's own interpretations to a validation group to receive the benefit of the mutual, rational controls of the intersubjective criticism of others (Popper, 1975, p. 44).

iii) Using action-reflection cycles in clarifying and evolving the energy-flowing and values-laden explanatory principles in generating knowledge about improving educational influences in learning.

In the process of expressing concerns when values are not being lived as fully as they could be, imagining possible improvements, choosing a possibility to act on, acting and gathering data and evaluating the influence of actions, the energy-flowing values used to distinguish what counts as an improvement are clarified and evolved. Clarifying these values is a necessary condition for judging whether improvements in learning are occurring. For example, at one time in my classrooms I felt that I was imposing too much structure on the lessons so that there was insufficient freedom to enable my pupils to engage in any enquiry learning that involved them forming their own questions. It was only by clarifying my understanding of enquiry learning and showing the development from a highly structured classroom to one that included the possibility of enquiry learning that I could clearly communicate what I meant by an improvement in learning (Whitehead, 1976).

iv) Using responses from validation groups to enhance the imagined possibilities for improving educational influences in learning and for improving the gathering of data to make a judgement on the effectiveness of the actions.

One of the best illustrations of this use of a validation group is in Martin Forrest's (1984) MA dissertation. As a tutor working in the continuing professional development of teachers, Forrest supported teachers to help their pupils to improve their learning. Forrest researched his educational influence with a teacher in helping some primary-age children to think historically with objects from a museum service. Another teacher working with similar-age pupils from a different school did not believe this thinking to be possible. For his first validation meeting, Forrest made claims to have influenced the practice of the first teacher but with insufficient evidence to convince the validation group of the validity of his claims. The validation group explained that they would need to see more conclusive evidence of his influence in the learning of a teacher and the pupils than he provided in his initial narrative.

At a validation group some months later, Forrest produced video evidence in his explanation of his influence showing that the second teacher, on being shown a videotape of what the first teacher was doing with her pupils, had tried the work with the historical artefacts. She found to her surprise that the pupils could think historically about the objects in a way that she initially had not thought to be possible. Forrest had documented his work with the second teacher. He had video-evidence from the classroom showing the pupils working with the artefacts and developing their historical thinking. His analysis with the video data convinced the group of the validity of his claims to know his educational influences in the learning of the teacher and pupils.

Forrest shows how the primacy of practice and of improving practice is not separated from the generation of knowledge. Here is how an individual's living-theory methodology can assist in the generation of knowledge.

d) Generating Knowledge With A Living-Theory Methodology

i) The importance of forming good questions.

As with improving practice, generating knowledge relies on asking, researching and answering good questions. At the present time there is much work to be done on establishing the appropriate epistemology for evaluating the quality of claims to educational knowledge from within a Living Theory perspective. So, I think good questions in the present can be focused on the expression, clarification, evolution and legitimation of living standards of judgement.

ii) Using action-reflection cycles in the generation of educational knowledge.

The generation of educational knowledge includes knowledge of a living-theory methodology. In the story of the growth of my educational knowledge my most recent contributions have focused on the explication of a living-theory methodology for improving practice and generating knowledge (Whitehead, 2009). In my analysis of an individual's educational development (Whitehead, 1985) I suggest that educational researchers adopt an action reflection form in generating a living form of theory:

The approach to educational theory I am suggesting we adopt rests on a number of assumptions concerning both the idea of a 'living form of theory' and the personal and social criteria which can be used to criticise the theory. I use the term a 'living form of theory' to distinguish the suggested approach from the 'linguistic form' in which traditional theories are presented for criticism. In a living approach to educational theory I am suggesting that teachers present their claims to know how and why they are attempting to overcome practical educational problems in this form:

- I experience a problem when some of my educational values are negated in my practice.
- I imagine a solution to my problem.

- I act in the direction of my solution.
- I evaluate the outcomes of my actions.
- I modify my problems, ideas and actions in the light of my evaluations (ibid, p. 98).

In creating their own living-theory methodology, an individual includes the unique constellation of values that they use to give meaning and purpose to their existence. In the course of the enquiry these values are expressed, clarified and evolved as explanatory principles in explanations of educational influences in learning. The values flow with a life-affirming energy and are expressed in the relational dynamics of educational relationships.

One of the tasks, for those interested in spreading the educational influence and academic legitimation of living-educational-theories and a living-theory methodology, is to find appropriate ways of representing the flows of life-affirming energy with values as explanatory principles in narratives of educational influences in learning. It is to find appropriate ways of engaging in the boundaries of the power relations that are both resistant and supportive of the legitimation of living theories and living-theory methodology. I have outlined above, the tensions I experienced in my early studies of educational theory.

The tensions arose because my practical principles were seen by adherents to the disciplines approach to educational theory as at best pragmatic maxims that had at best a crude and superficial justification in practice and which would be replaced in any rationally justified theory. Similar tensions continue because the majority of renowned and internationally recognised journals of educational research continue to be text-based rather than web-based and eliminate multimedia representations from their contents. Hence my tension in seeing that visual representations of flows of life-affirming energy with values are being eliminated from journals of educational research.

iii) Using multimedia representations to clarify and share meanings of the flows of energy in embodied values and their expressions in explanations of educational influence in learning.

I am suggesting that we are all living with the capacity to express and develop a relationally dynamic awareness of space and boundaries with life-affirming energy and value. However, I am also claiming that the dominating forms of representation used in universities for explaining educational practices and influences in learning remove valid expressions of this energy with values, from the explanations. I am claiming that the forms of representation that dominate printed text-based media cannot express adequately, in the standards of judgement and explanatory principles of academic texts, the embodied values we use to give meaning and purpose to our lives in education.

I believe that the reason for this removal lies in the continuing tendency of academic theories to replace the practical principles used by individuals to explain their lives, by principles with justifications in abstract rationality. What I am saying we should be creating is educational theories from a perspective of inclusionality developed by Rayner and Lumley:

> At the heart of inclusionality… is a simple shift in the way we frame reality, from absolutely fixed to relationally dynamic. This shift arises from perceiving space and boundaries as connective, reflective and co-creative, rather than severing, in their vital role of producing heterogeneous form and local identity… To make this shift does not depend on new scientific knowledge or conjecture about supernatural forces, extraterrestrial life or whatever. All it requires is awareness and assimilation into understanding of the spatial possibility that permeates within, around and through natural features from sub-atomic to Universal in scale. We can then see through the illusion of 'solidity' that has made us prone to regard 'matter' as 'everything' and 'space' as 'nothing', and hence get caught in the conceptual addiction and affliction of 'either/or' 'dualism'. An addiction that so powerfully and insidiously restricts our philosophical horizons and undermines our compassionate human spirit and creativity (Rayner, 2004).

I want to highlight the importance of understanding that, from a perspective of inclusionality, we are all included in the dynamics of a common living space that flows with life-affirming energy. As Ted Lumley, one of the originators of the idea of inclusionality, points out about the importance of recognising a 'pooling-of-consciousness':

> … an inspiring pooling-of-consciousness that seems to include and connect all within all in unifying dynamical communion…. The concreteness of 'local object being'… allows us to understand the dynamics of the common living-space in which we are all ineluctably included participants (Lumley, 2008, p. 3).

Working with such a relationally dynamic awareness of space and boundaries does not mean that everything is to be included in an undifferentiated mush. The living boundaries of cultures in resistance sometimes include the need for protection against damaging influences, especially those involving a lack of recognition (Whitehead, 2008c).

In learning how to combine our voices as practitioner-researchers in the generation and testing of living-educational-theories I am aware of the importance of including narrative wreckage in the story of a life well-lived. I am thinking of the kind of narrative wreckage that involves a lack of recognition. A smooth story of self might initially feel comfortable to a listener, but without the acknowledgement of what has been involved in persisting in the face of pressure, a story can lack authenticity (Whitehead and Delong, 2008).

In my experience most lives involve some form of narrative wreckage in which difficulties have been encountered that require some effort in rechannelling destructive emotions into a flow of life-affirming energy. I am thinking particularly of rechannelling destructive responses to a lack of appropriate recognition. I am thinking of the development of protective boundaries, in the face of such violations, that can continue to be open to the flow of life-affirming energy and values that carry hope for the future of humanity:

> Human beings seek recognition of their own worth, or of the people, things, or principles that they invest with worth. The desire for recognition, and the accompanying emotions of anger, shame and pride, are parts of the human personality critical to political life. According to Hegel, they are what drive the whole historical process (Fukuyama, 1992, p. xvii).

In overcoming and circumventing obstacles to the flows of energy with values of humanity I feel that two affirmations have been most significant in my practitioner-research:

> The first affirmation is the experience of an energy that I feel is flowing through the cosmos. This energy is life-affirming for me and I associate this energy with the state of being affirmed by the power of being itself. When I read these words in Paul Tillich's work in *The Courage To Be* (1962, p. 168), I understood that this affirmation referred to a theistic experience in a relationship with God. Having no theistic desires myself, I use the words 'state of being affirmed by the power of being itself' to communicate my experience of a flow of life-affirming energy that when combined with my values provides me with explanatory principles to explain why I do what I do. I believe that a similar energy is informing an Ubuntu way of being as this is expressed by Nelson Mandela and brought into the Academy by Charles (2007) as a living standard of judgement in his doctoral thesis. I also identify this energy with Joan Walton's living standard of judgement in her doctoral thesis of "spiritual resilience gained through connection with a loving dynamic energy (Walton, 2008, abstract).

The second affirmation is in relationships with others when mutual recognition evokes a flow of life-affirming energy. One event in which I experienced this affirmation was on the evening of Jacqueline Delong's graduation day on 18 December 2002, when Peter Mellett led a celebration for Jacqueline in the Department of Education of the University of Bath. I believe that you will feel this affirmation 32 seconds into the video clip when the laughter bursts out (Video 1).

Video 1. Peter Mellett celebrating on Jacqueline Delong's graduation (Whitehead, 2006a)

https://www.youtube.com/watch?fmt=6&gl=GB&hl=en-GB&v=HxqRF2tVLB4.

To communicate my meanings of the importance of a life-affirming energy and values such as academic freedom, pleasure, humour, love and justice in explanations of educational influence I shall use two multimedia representations. The first is a video of a keynote to the International Conference of Teacher Research in New York in March 2008, on Combining voices in living-educational-theories that are freely given in Teacher Research (Whitehead, 2008b, 2008c). In presenting the keynote I felt that I was loving what I was doing. Such keynotes offer the opportunity to communicate ideas from my research programme that are directly related to what it has meant to me to live a loving and productive life in education. The following video clip shows me using multimedia to explain the importance of visual representations to communicate flows of life-affirming energy and loving recognition in explanations of educational influences in learning (Video 2).

Video 2. Jack Whitehead's keynote ICTR 08 clip 1 (Whitehead, 2008e)

https://www.youtube.com/watch?v=gWabP2acxfk&fmt=6.

I am using the following video clip (see Video 3) from the keynote to show a form of spiritual resilience gained through connection with a loving dynamic energy (Walton, 2008). The video shows me, to myself, responding to the living memories of the most difficult experiences of my working life. In these responses I am hopeful that you experience the flow of loving energy with pleasure, humour and a passion for knowledge-creation that I feel distinguish my educational relationships and explanations of educational influence.

Video 3. Jack Whitehead's keynote ICTR 08 clip 2 (Whitehead, 2008f)

https://www.youtube.com/watch?v=KXLqGAAK-D0&fmt=6.

As I watch this video clip I see myself expressing a loving energy, pleasure, humour and understanding as I describe judgements from the university that generated the most difficult experiences of my working life. My purpose in including them in my accounts of my educational journey and knowledge-creation is to avoid presenting a smooth story of self that contains no narrative wreckage. In my experience of listening to many life histories, everyone has encountered difficulties that have required spiritual resilience and a connection with a loving energy to move beyond the difficulties. Scholes-Rhodes (2002) has expressed her experience of spiritual belonging as a sense of 'exquisite connectivity'. She creates an 'intricate patterning of personal stories and dialogical enquiry process in forming a sense of coherence from the juxtaposition of emotional images with the clarity of a reflective and cognitive dialogue' (abstract, 2002). The coherence I am seeking is one which includes emotional difficulties as 'exquisite connectivity' is broken, denied and re-established.

With the exception of the experience of 2006 described below, I have documented most of the difficulties experienced over the 30 years between 1976 and 2006 in previous publications (Whitehead, 1993, 2004). They include a 1976 judgement by the university that I had exhibited forms of behaviour that had harmed the good order and morale of the School of Education. They include the 1980 and 1982 judgements that I could not question the judgements of examiners of my two doctoral submissions under any circumstances. They include the 1987 judgement that my activities and writings were a challenge to the present and proper order of the university and not consistent with the duties the university wished me to pursue.

In 1990, based on this judgement about my activities and writings, as evidence of a prima facie breach of my academic freedom, Senate established a working party on a matter of academic freedom. They reported in 1991: 'The working party did not find that... his academic freedom had actually been breached. This was however, because of Mr. Whitehead's persistence in the face of pressure; a less determined individual might well have been discouraged and therefore constrained.'

Video 4. Responding to matters of power and academic freedom (Whitehead, 2006b)

https://www.youtube.com/watch?v=MBTLfyjkFh0&fmt=6.

Here is my re-enactment of a meeting with the working party where I had been invited to respond to a draft report in which the conclusion was that my academic freedom had not been breached, a conclusion I agreed with. What I did not agree with was that there was no recognition of the pressure to which I had been subjected while sustaining my academic freedom. In the clip I think you may feel a disturbing shock in the recognition of the power of my anger in the expression of energy and my passion for academic freedom and academic responsibility. Following my meeting with the working party the report that went to Senate acknowledged that the reason my academic freedom had not been breached was because of my persistence in the face of pressure. This phrase, 'persistence in the face of pressure', is a phrase I continue to use in comprehending my meaning of

Walton's standard of judgement of spiritual resilience gained through connection with a loving dynamic energy (Walton, 2008).

I have included this video clip on the grounds of authenticity. To understand the educational significance of the video of my keynote of March 2008, in my explanations of educational influence, requires an understanding of the significance of the rechannelling of the energy in the anger in the above video. I expressed this rechannelling in the keynote. This rechannelling was related to persistence in the face of pressure. This persistence was possible through remaining open to the flows of loving dynamic energy in the passion for improving practice and contributing to educational knowledge.

Whilst much valuable learning can take place in response to difficulties, I do want to emphasise the importance of the affirmations of those I have worked with in generating their own living-educational-theories, in sustaining my own passion for education. These affirmations are expressed most delightfully by Spiro in the story epilogue of her thesis, Learning and teacher as fellow travellers: a story tribute to Jack Whitehead (Spiro, 2008, p. xv:

http://www.actionresearch.net/living/janespiropdfphd/storyepilogue.pdf).

This flows with a loving recognition, respectful connectedness and educational responsibility (Huxtable, 2008). These help to sustain my own loving relations and productive life in education.

One of the greatest difficulties I have experienced in remaining open to a flow of loving energy for education is in responding to a lack of recognition of my contributions to educational knowledge. This lack of recognition has been sustained over the 30 years 1976-2006 in judgements made about these contributions in the university. The latest judgement was in 2006 with the rejection of my application for a Readership on the grounds that I needed to develop my case further by focusing on producing articles which can be disseminated via established and renowned international refereed journals. Bruce Ferguson (2008), Whitehead (2008a), Laidlaw (2008) and Adler-Collins (2008) have all made a case in the British Educational Research Association publication, Research Intelligence, to explain why the forms of representation in established and renowned international refereed journals need extending to include the new forms of educational knowledge being communicated through EJOLTS. EJOLTS is being established because the existing established and renowned international refereed journals are not providing appropriate forms of representation for the communication of living-educational-theories. Laidlaw's (2008) contribution is particularly significant in communicating meanings of living standards of judgement because she includes live urls in the e-version of Research Intelligence. These take readers directly to the work of Branko Bognar (2008a, 2008b) with teachers and pupils in classrooms in Croatia, as well as to educational relationships with Moira Laidlaw's students in China.

We can all help each other, whatever age, to create our own living-educational-theories in which we account to ourselves for living our values and understandings as fully as we can. You can see at

http://www.actionresearch.net/writings/mastermod.shtml

the living-theories of master educators, and at

http://www.actionresearch.net/living/living.shtml

the living-theories of doctor educators that have been freely given for sharing through the internet, in the hope that they will contribute ideas that may be of value in the generation of your living-theories as we combine our voices in enhancing our educational influences in improving our local and global contexts.

As I write I am feeling the pleasure of anticipation that this contribution will be accepted for publication in *EJOLTS* and hence become publicly available. I am sharing these ideas with you in the hope that you will find something of value for yourself that resonates with your own life-affirming energy, values and understandings.

In conclusion I want to briefly focus attention on the importance of acting locally and publishing our ideas globally in ways that can support national and international collaborations.

iv) *Developing national and international collaborations for improving practice and generating educational knowledge*

My experiences of Action Researchers from different countries include Action Research workshops and presentations in China, Japan, Australia, Malaysia, the Republic of Ireland, South Africa, the UK, the USA and Canada. The workshops and presentations have helped me to recognise the importance of understanding the normative backgrounds of different cultures (Whitehead, 2008, c, f, g, h). I recognise that the emphasis placed on collective identities in China and Japan is different to the emphasis placed on individual identity in Australia, Ireland, the UK, the USA and Canada. Western views of democracy, which influence my own identity, have been questioned by Islamic scholars:

> There exists in Islam a mechanism for consulting the believers, the Shura, which is an integral part of Islam. However, the system in Western democracy whereby the majority decides what is lawful and what is not, can never be acceptable in Islam, where the laws and framework of society are revealed by Allah and are unchangeable (Abdul-Rahman, 1982, p. 35).

Whatever our sociocultural history I believe that educators around the world have a responsibility to enhance the flow of values and understandings that carry hope for the future of humanity. This involves sharing our different understandings of what constitutes a good social formation and which values and understandings carry hope for the future of humanity.

For example, Jane Spiro (2008) in her research into knowledge-transformation engages with her own creativity as a creative writer, educator, manager and educational researcher. She holds herself to account in her thesis and research programme in relation to the values and understandings that she believes carry hope for the future of humanity. By making public her thesis with these values and understandings, in the flow of communications through web space, Spiro is fulfilling one of the fundamental responsibilities of an educational researcher. I am thinking of the responsibility to engage in systematic enquiry that is made public. In her thesis, produced locally, through her research at Oxford Brookes University, Spiro explains how the embodied knowledge of a writer, educator, manager and researcher can be made public, in a distinct academic approach that includes the exercise of creativity and narrative enquiry in the generation of a living-educational-theory. This thesis is now available through the international communication channels of the internet

(http://www.actionresearch.net/living/janespirophd.shtml).

It is my belief that the insights in this thesis, about how to make public the embodied knowledge of a practitioner-researcher, will travel across cultural boundaries to captivate the imaginations and practices of others.

You can see how this kind of communication has already moved across cultural and national boundaries in the work of Dean Tian Fengjun and Professor Moira Laidlaw (Fengjun and Laidlaw, 2006) with their colleagues, in China's Experimental Centre for Educational Action Research in Foreign Languages Teaching, at Ningxia Teachers University. The Action Researchers at Ningxia Teachers University are developing a collaborative approach to Living Theory Action Research with Chinese characteristics. You can access the living-theories of teachers and students about their learning and implementation of the New Curriculum at Ningxia Teachers University from

http://actionresearch.net/writings/moira.shtml.

You can also access some of my suggestions for international collaborations in the development of collaborative Living Theory Action Research in China from

http://www.actionresearch.net/writings/jack/jwkeynotechina8june08.pdf.

Dr. Margaret Farren and her colleague Yvonne Crotty at Dublin City University are evolving their living-theory action research approach for improving practice and generating knowledge with information and communications technology. Dr. Farren is a lecturer in e-learning at Dublin City University who is working to support international collaboration with the Action Research Collaboratory and the eLife Connecting People Project.

Professor Jean McNiff has been most influential through books, workshops and conference presentations in spreading the influence of a Living Theory Action Research approach. This influence can be seen particularly through her work in South Africa (Wood, Morar and Mostert, 2007), in Ireland, Iceland, Canada, and in the UK.

I want to end with references to photographs from graduation ceremonies in 2008 from Limerick University and the University of Bath to symbolise the spreading global influence of the living-theories of individuals produced in their local contexts.

In a picture taken in January 2008 (University of Limerick, 2008) Jean McNiff is in her doctoral robes from the University of Bath celebrating the success of Margaret Cahill and Mary Roche on their graduations with their living theories doctorates from the University of Limerick. The symbolism of the robes in relation to ideas travelling through national boundaries is that ideas generated by McNiff in her doctoral research programme at the University of Bath have been integrated in the living-theory doctorates of Cahill and Roche at the University of Limerick.

Jean McNiff has supervised three other living-theory doctorates (Glenn, 2006; Sullivan, 2006; McDonagh, 2007) to successful completion at the University of Limerick with graduations in 2006 and 2007, and more are on the way. The explicit embrace of enhancing the expression of the values of social justice and holistic educational practice in the theses provide evidence of an educational engagement with issues of power and privilege in society.

Image 1 below shows myself on the left, with Jane Spiro and Je Kan Adler-Collins on their graduation with their doctorates on 25 June 2008. We three are alumni of the University of Bath. Ideas from my research programme have been integrated within the theses of Spiro and Adler-Collins as they generated their own original living-educational-theories. Adler-Collins' research programme involved the development, implementation and evaluation of a curriculum for the healing nurse in a Japanese university. Spiro's research programme includes family history from Poland where in Chapter 4 of her thesis on Writing as finding a voice: From Finchley to Lithuania. She writes:

> This chapter explores my novel-writing process, the struggle to understand the actual life stories/histories of those I grew up with, and to honour this specificity, at the same time as transforming it symbolically into a larger, and 'universal' story (Spiro, 2008, p. 82).

Image 1. Jack Whitehead, with Jane Spiro and Je Kan
Adler-Collins on graduation day.

The image brings back the memory of the expression of life-affirming energy, pleasure, hope and friendship between us. The supervision relationship has now changed to one of doctoral colleagues in our three universities who are supporting each other in our post-doctoral research. The process of researching our actions locally and publishing our research globally continues with the extending interconnecting and branching channels of our communications. I do hope that you will feel moved to contribute your own living-educational-theory to our educational journeys in our shared living space.

Margaret Cahill's (2007) thesis is on *My Living Educational Theory Of Inclusional Practice*, and Mary Roche's (2007) thesis is on *Towards A Living Theory Of Caring Pedagogy: Interrogating My Practice To Nurture A Critical, Emancipatory And Just Community Of Enquiry.*

References

Abdul-Rahman S.A. (1982) *Educational Theory: A Qur'anic Outlook*. Makkah, Saudi Arabia: Umm Al-Qura University.

Adler-Collins, J. (2008) Creating New Forms Of Living Educational Theories Through Collaborative Educational Research From Eastern And Western Contexts: A response to Jack Whitehead. *Research Intelligence*, 104; 17–18.

Adler-Collins, J. (2007) *Developing An Inclusional Pedagogy Of The Unique: How Do I Clarify, Live And Explain My Educational Influences In My Learning As I Pedagogise My Healing Nurse Curriculum In A Japanese University?* PhDl thesis, University of Bath. Retrieved 28 January 2008, from http://www.actionresearch.net/living/jekan.shtml.

Allender, J. and Allender, D.S. (2008) *The Humanistic Teacher: First the Child, Then Curriculum*. Boulder: Paradigm Publishers.

Bernstein. B. (2000) *Pedagogy, Symbolic Control and Identity: Theory, Research, Critique*. Lanham, Boulder, New York, Oxford: Rowman & Littlefield.

Bourdieu, P. (1990). *The Logic of Practice*. Stanford, CA: Stanford University Press.

Bognar, B. (2008b, 25 June) Pupil – action researchers [video file]. Posted to http://www.vimeo.com/1230806.

Bognar, B. (2008b, 27 July) *Validation of pupil's action research report* [video file]. Posted to http://www.vimeo.com/1415387.

Bruce Ferguson, P. (2008) Increasing Inclusion in Educational Research: Reflections from New Zealand. *Research Intelligence*, 102, 24–25.

Charles, E. (2007) How Can I Bring Ubuntu As A Living Standard Of Judgement Into The Academy? Moving Beyond Decolonisation Through Societal Re-Identification And Guiltless Recognition. PhD thesis, University of Bath. Retrieved 10 September 2008, from: http://www.actionresearch.net/edenphd.shtml.

Collingwood, R.G. (1991) *An Autobiography*. Oxford: Oxford University Press.

Farren, M. (2008). The eLife Connecting People Project. Retrieved 29 September 2008, from http://www.jackwhitehead.com/farren/eLife.htm.

Fukuyama, F. (1992) *The End of History and the Last Man*. London: Penguin.

Glenn, M. (2006) *Working With Collaborative Projects: My Living Theory Of A Holistic Educational Practice*. PhD thesis, University of Limerick. Retrieved 29 September 2008, from http://www.jeanmcniff.com/glennabstract.html.

Habermas, J. (1976) *Communication and the Evolution of Society*. London: Heinemann.

Hirst, P. (Ed.) (1983) *Educational Theory and Its Foundation Disciplines*. London: Routledge and Kegan Paul.

Huxtable, J. (2008, September) *How Do I Improve My Educational Practice As I Support Educators Who Are Developing Inclusive And Inclusional Theory And Practice Of Gifts And Talents Whilst Responding To National Developments?* Paper presented at the British Educational Research Association Annual Conference, Edinburgh, Scotland.

Ilyenkov, E. (1977) *Dialectical Logic*. Moscow: Progress Publishers.

Laidlaw, M. (2008) Increasing Inclusion In Educational Research: A Response To Pip Bruce Ferguson and Jack Whitehead. *Research Intelligence*, 104; 16–17.

Laidlaw, M. (2006) *How Might We Enhance the Educational Value of our Research-base at the New University in Guyuan? Researching Stories for the Social Good* (Inaugural Professorial Lecture). Retrieved 22 September 2008, from http://www.actionresearch.net/writings/china/mlinaugural.pdf.

Laidlaw, M. (1996) *How Can I Create My Own Living-Educational-Theory As I Account For My Educational Development?* (PhD thesis, University of Bath, 1996). Retrieved 10 September 2008, from http://www.actionresearch.net/living/moira2.shtml.

Lumley, T. (2008) *A Fluid-Dynamical World View*. Victoria, British Columbia: Printorium Bookworks.

MacDonald, B. (1976) Evaluation and control of education. In D.A. Tawney (Ed.) *Curriculum Evaluation Today: Trends and Implications* (pp. 125–136). London: Macmillan Education.

Marcuse, H. (1964) *One Dimensional Man*. London: Routledge and Kegan Paul.

McDonagh, C. (2007) *My Living Theory Of Learning To Teach For Social Justice: How Do I Enable Primary School Children With Specific Learning Disability (Dyslexia) And Myself*

As Their Teacher To Realise Our Learning Potentials? (PhD Thesis, University of Limerick, 2007). Retrieved 29 September 2008, from: http://www.jeanmcniff.com/items.asp?id=48.

McNiff, J. and Whitehead, J. (2006) *All You Need To Know About Action Research*. London: SAGE.

McNiff, J. and Whitehead, J. (2008) *Evaluating Quality in Doing and Writing Action Research in Schools, Neighbourhoods and Communities: AERA professional Development Training and Extended Courses Proposal*. Retrieved 3 March 2008 from http://www.actionresearch.net/writings/aeraictr08/jmjwaeraprofdev08.htm.

McVeigh, B. (2002) *Japanese Higher Education as Myth*. New York: M.E. Sharpe.

Mellett, P. (2006, 5 December) *Celebrating Jackie Delong's Graduation* [video file]. Posted to http://uk.youtube.com/watch?v=HxqRF2tVLB4.

Murray, Y.P. (2007) *How I Develop A Cosmopolitan Academic Practice In Moving Through Narcissistic Injury With Educational Responsibility: A Contribution To An Epistemology And Methodology Of Educational Knowledge*. (Doctoral submission to the University of Bath, 2007).

Polanyi, M. (1958) *Personal Knowledge: Towards a Post-Critical Philosophy*. London: Routledge and Kegan Paul.

Popper, K. (1975) *The Logic of Scientific Discovery*. London: Hutchinson & Co.

Rayner, A. (2004) *Inclusionality: The Science, Art and Spirituality of Place, Space and Evolution*. Retrieved 6 July 2008 from http://opus.bath.ac.uk/25117/ (not available).

Ryle, G. (1973) *The Concept of Mind*. Harmondsworth: Penguin.

Said, E. (1993) *Culture and Imperialism*. London: Vintage.

Scholes-Rhodes, J. (2002) *From The Inside Out: Learning To Presence My Aesthetic And Spiritual Being Through The Emergent Form Of A Creative Art Of Inquiry*. (PhD thesis, University of Bath, 2002). Retrieved 10 September 2008, from http://www.actionresearch.net/living/rhodes.shtml.

Schön, D. (1995) The New Scholarship Requires a New Epistemology. *Change*, 27(6); 27–34.

Schütz, A. (1972) *The Phenomenology of the Social World*. London: Heinemann.

Sen, A. (1999) *Development as Freedom*. Oxford: Oxford University Press.

Smith, C.A. (2003) Supporting Teacher And School Development: Learning And Teaching Policies, Shared Living Theories And Teacher-Researcher Partnerships. *Teacher Development*, 6(2); 157–179.

Spiro, J. (2008) *How I Have Arrived At A Notion Of Knowledge Transformation, Through Understanding The Story Of Myself As Creative Writer, Creative Educator, Creative Manager, And Educational Researcher*. PhD thesis, University of Bath. Retrieved 14 July 2008 from http://www.actionresearch.net/living/janespirophd.shtml.

Sullivan, B. (2006) *A Living Theory Of A Practice Of Social Justice: Realising The Right Of Traveller Children To Educational Equality*. PhD thesis, University of Limerick, 2006. Retrieved 10 December 2008 from http://www.jeanmcniff.com/items.asp?id=47.

Thomas, G. and Gorard, S. (2007) Quality in Education Research. *International Journal of Research & Method in Education*, 30(3); 239–242.

Tian, F. and Laidlaw, M. (2006) *Action Research and the Foreign Languages Teaching*. Xi'an, P.R. China: Shaanxi Tourism Publishing House.

Tillich, P. (1962) *The Courage To Be*. London: Fontana.

University of Limerick. (2008) University of Limerick Winter Conferrings 2008. Retrieved 9 September 2008 from http://www2.ul.ie/web/WWW/Services/News?did=721750371&pageUrl=/WWW/Services/News.

Walton, J. (2008) *Ways of Knowing: Can I find a way of knowing that satisfies my search for meaning?* PhD thesis, University of Bath.

Whitehead, J. (1972) *A Way To Professionalism In Education*. MA dissertation, University of London, 1972.

Whitehead, J. (1976) *Improving Learning For 11–14-Year-Olds In Mixed Ability Science Groups*. Swindon: Wiltshire Curriculum Development Centre.

Whitehead, J. (1985) An Analysis Of An Individual's Educational Development – The Basis For Personally Orientated Action Research. In Shipman, M. (Ed.) *Educational Research: Principles, Policies & Practices* (pp. 97–108). London: Falmer.

Whitehead, J. (1989) Creating a Living Educational Theory from Questions of the Kind, 'How Do I Improve my Practice?' *Cambridge Journal of Education*, 19(1), 41–52.

Whitehead, J. (1993) *The Growth of Educational Knowledge: Creating Your Own Living Educational Theories*. Bournemouth: Hyde.

Whitehead, J. (2004) Do Action Researchers' Expeditions Carry Hope For The Future Of Humanity? How Do We Know? Action Research Expeditions, October 2004. Retrieved 8 July 2008, from http://www.actionresearch.net/writings/jack/jwareoct04.pdf.

Whitehead, J. (2006a, 5 December) *Peter Mellett celebrating on Jacqueline Delong's Graduation* [video file]. Posted to http://uk.youtube.com/watch?v=HxqRF2tVLB4

Whitehead, J. (2006b, 30 December) *Responding to matters of power and academic freedom* [video file].

Whitehead, J. (2008a) Increasing Inclusion In Educational Research: A Response To Pip Bruce Ferguson. *Research Intelligence*, 103; 16–17.

Whitehead, J. (2008b, March) *Combining Voices In Living Educational Theories That Are Freely Given In Teacher Research*. Keynote presentation for the International Conference of Teacher Research on Combining Voices in Teacher Research, New York, USA. Retrieved from http://www.actionresearch.net/writings/aerictr08/jwictr08key.htm.

Whitehead, J. (2008c) *Keynote presentation for the International Conference of Teacher Research on Combining Voices in Teacher Research*, New York [video file]. Posted to mms://wms.bath.ac.uk/live/education/JackWhitehead_030408/jackkeynoteictr280308large.wmv.

Whitehead, J. (2008d, March) *How Are Living Educational Theories Being Produced And Legitimated In The Boundaries Of Cultures In Resistance?* Paper presented at the Cultures in Resistance Conference of the Discourse, Power, Resistance Series, Manchester UK. Retrieved from http://www.actionresearch.net/writings/jack/jwmanchester170308.htm.

Whitehead, J. (2008e, 27 August) *Jack Whitehead's keynote ICTR 08 clip 1* [video file]. Posted to http://www.youtube.com/watch?v=gWabP2acxfk.

Whitehead, J. (2008f, 27 August) *Jack Whitehead's keynote ICTR 08 clip 2* [video file]. Posted to http://www.youtube.com/watch?v=KXLqGAAK-D0.

Whitehead, J. (2008g, March) *How Can S-STEP Research Contribute to the Enhancement of Civic Responsibility in Schools, Neighborhoods, and Communities?* Paper presented in the session: Becoming Innovative Through Self-Study Research, at the 2008 Annual Conference of the American Educational Research Association, New York, USA. Retrieved 3 March 2008, from http://www.actionresearch.net/writings/jack/jwmanchester170308.htm.

Whitehead, J. (2008h, March) *How Can I- We Create Living Educational Theories From Research Into Professional Learning?* Paper presented in the symposium convened by Jean McNiff on Communicating and testing the validity of claims to transformational systemic influence for civic responsibility, at AERA, New York, USA. Retrieved from http://www.actionresearch.net/writings/jack/jwaera08jmsem.htm .

Whitehead, J. (2008i, June) *Collaborative Living Educational Theory Action Research in China.* Keynote presented at a conference of China's Experimental Centre for Educational Action Research in Foreign Languages Teacher, Ningxia, China. Retrieved from http://www.actionresearch.net/writings/jack/jwkeynotechina8june08.pdf .

Whitehead, J. (2009) How Do I Influence The Generation Of Living Educational Theories For Personal And Social Accountability In Improving Practice? In Tidwell, D., Heston, M. and Fitzgerald, L. (Eds.) *Research Methods for the Self-Study of Practice.* New York: Springer.

Whitehead, J. and Delong, J. (2008, March) *Persisting In The Face Of Pressures: How Have We Contributed To The Generation Of Cultures Of Inquiry?* Paper presented at the International Conference of Teacher Research (ICTR) 2008 with the Theme: Combining Voices: Building a Teacher Research Community. New York, USA. Retrieved from http://www.leeds.ac.uk/educol/documents/172701.htm .

Whitehead, J. and McNiff, J. (2006) *Action Research Living Theory.* London: SAGE.

Wood, L.A., Morar, R. and Mostert, L. (2007) From rhetoric to reality: the role of Living Theory Action Research. *Education as Change*, 11(2); 67–80.

Yunus, M. (2007) *Creating a World Without Poverty: Social Business and the Future of Capitalism.* New York: Public Affairs.

PAPER FIVE.

Generating Educational Theories That Can Explain Educational Influences in Learning. **Presented in the keynote symposium on Explicating A New Epistemology For Educational Knowledge With Educational Responsibility at the British Educational Research Association Annual Conference on 3 September 2009 at the University of Manchester.**

This presentation continues the epistemological emphasis in Paper Three within a community of researchers that are united around the theme of the symposium of explicating a new epistemology for educational knowledge with educational responsibility. This paper presents the units of appraisal, the living standards of judgement, and the living logics that help to constitute living-educational-theories with educational responsibility. It explains the significance of grounding the epistemology in communities of practice with individuals accepting the responsibility of seeing themselves as knowledge-creation as they explain their educational influences in learning. The meanings of the practical principles that can constitute explanations of educational influence are clarified using digital technology in multimedia narratives.

The importance of a method of empathetic resonance is introduced, using digital visual data to point, with precision, to the expressions of the meanings of the energy-flowing, ontological and relational values that individual Living Theory researchers are using to give meaning and purpose to their lives.

The practical principles used in the process of knowledge-creation are understood to exist within communities of practice and ecologies of knowledges. The living-theories of five Irish researchers, accredited by the University of Limerick between 1995 and 1996, are pointed towards to emphasise the importance of communities of practice in the generation and spreading influence of living-educational-theories and Living Theory research.

The understanding of the living standards of judgement is deepened and extended with the help of Alan Rayner's idea of inclusionality, as a relationally dynamic awareness of space and boundaries that are connective, reflexive and co-creative. The importance of living-logic in clarified in Paper Five, with the importance of reflexivity providing a focus for Paper Six.

PAPER FIVE.

Generating Educational Theories That Can Explain Educational Influences in Learning

Abstract

For centuries, the knowledge that has been used to enhance professionalism in education has been presented to the Academy for legitimation in bound volumes of mainly words on pages of printed text. The language and logics of these texts have been dominated by the Aristotelian logic with its law of contradiction to eliminate contradictions from correct thought, and to a lesser extent by a dialectical logic with the inclusion of the nucleus of contradiction in correct thought. In these texts, educational theory is presented within conceptual frameworks in which explanations for the educational influences of individuals in learning are tested for validity through the application of an explanation, derived from the general explanation in the theory, to a particular case.

Different forms of explanation are offered here to enhance professionalism and generate educational knowledge. These explanations are grounded in the belief that the embodied knowledge of many educators could be made explicit to recognise the accomplishments of master and doctor educators. The explanations are generated by individuals in enquiries of the kind, 'How do I improve what I am doing?', working within communities of practice and knowledge-creation.

The explanations offered below include multimedia presentations using digital technology to look at the practical principles in the explanations given by individuals for their educational influences in learning. The practical principles are grounded in energy-flowing values with an awareness of the influence of the relational dynamics of complex ecologies (Lee and Rochon, 2009). I call such explanations living-educational theories to distinguish them from the theories of education derived from the traditional disciplines of education.

The primary contribution of these presentations to the theme of the symposium is in the explication of the units of appraisal, standards of judgement and living logics in an epistemology for living-educational-theories with educational responsibility.

Introduction

As a student of education between 1966 and 1967, on my initial teacher education programme at Newcastle University, I produced my first study of education entitled 'The way to professionalism in education?' My interest and passion in contributing to enhancing professionalism in education have continued with a sustained focus on the creation of educational theories that can validly explain the educational influences of individuals in their own learning, in the learning of others, and in the learning of social formations.

This presentation draws on my learning from a 36-year-old educational research programme into the nature of educational theory at the University of Bath between 1973 and 2009. It has particular significance for me because my tenured contract with the University was completed earlier this week on 31 August and I began a new three-year contract as a Visiting Fellow on 1 September. Hence, I can now start this new phase of my educational research at this keynote symposium with a review of my learning about educational theory over the course of my research programme.

Participating with me (Whitehead, 2009c) in this symposium are Margaret Farren from Dublin City University in the Chair, Christine Jones, an inclusion officer from Bath and North East Somerset as discussant, and Jean McNiff (2009) from York St John University, and Jane Renowden (2009) from St. Mary's College, and Marie Huxtable (2009b), a senior educational psychologist from Bath and North East Somerset, as co-presenters. We have worked together over several years and shared ideas in what I see as a community of practice and knowledge-creation.

In organising this presentation I shall:

1. Explain the significance of grounding it in communities of practice and knowledge-creation.
2. Give reasons for focusing on educational influences in learning with educational responsibility.
3. Present meanings of the practical principles that can constitute explanations of educational influence using digital technology in multimedia narratives.
4. Present the units of appraisal, the living standards of judgement and the living logics that help to constitute living-educational-theories with educational responsibility.

1. The Significance Of Communities Of Practice And Knowledge-Creation

My educational research programme has always been grounded in communities of practice and knowledge-creation. It originated in a conflict I experienced in 1971 whilst studying educational theory at the Institute of Education of the University of London and teaching full-time as a Head of the Science Department of Erkenwald Comprehensive School in Barking. My studies of educational theory on the Academic Diploma programme were influenced by the view that educational theory was constituted by the philosophy, sociology, psychology and history of education. This continued into my studies for the MA in the psychology of education between 1970 and 1972. This 'disciplines' approach to educational theory was generated and sustained by a community of practice and knowledge-creation at the Institute. However, in 1971 I began to question this assumption of the 'disciplines' approach to educational theory. No matter how I applied the conceptual frameworks of the disciplines of education, individually or in any combination, something was missing from the explanations. I could not derive from these theories a valid explanation for my educational influences in my own learning and in the learning of my pupils.

Reading Polanyi's (1958) *Personal Knowledge* helped me to understand that what was missing was my explanation for my educational influences in learning as I asked, researched and answered my question, 'How do I improve what I am doing?' Having recognised this error in my assumptions about educational theory I came to the University of Bath in 1973 to see if I could contribute to the creation of forms of educational theory that could produce valid explanations of educational influences in learning.

In recognising the importance of communities of practice and knowledge-creation in the generation of valid explanations, I want to stress the importance of the theme of the 2010 American Educational Research Association Conference on Understanding Complex Ecologies In A Changing World.

In a paper proposal for this AERA conference entitled Understanding Complex Ecologies In A Changing World For Improving Practice And Generating Educational Knowledge, Jean McNiff and I (Whitehead and McNiff, 2009) explain the importance of recognising the importance of complex ecologies and diverse cultural influences in explanations of educational influences in learning. We take our lead from Lee and Rochon's introduction to the theme for AERA 2010 where they say that:

> ... opportunities to learn within and across both formal and informal settings occur in the complex ecologies of people's lives, not isolated in a single setting such as a school or family. These complex ecologies include people's participation within and across multiple settings, from families to peer and intergenerational social networks, to schools and a variety of community organizations; and participation within and across these settings may be either physical or virtual (Lee and Rochon, 2009).

To help with the communication of the significance of a relationally dynamic awareness in explanatory principles that have been influenced by participation across different settings, here are some still images leading to video clips of each of the participants in the symposium. These are intended to show our embodied expressions of energy-flowing values, as explanatory principles in different contexts that are influenced by unique constellations of historical and sociocultural pressures. For example, when I make a claim below to know something about the explanatory principles Chris Jones uses to explain her influences as Inclusion Officer, I will draw your attention to the historical influence of an experience of 'feeling mortified', from Chris' primary school, in her decision to become a teacher with a passion for relating to pupils 'in the right way'. The diversity of influences from our sociocultural contexts embraces our work in the UK, the Republic of Ireland, the USA and South Africa.

What I want to accomplish in showing you the visual data below is to focus your attention on the diversity of our historical and sociocultural contexts and the complexity of the ecological influences that may need to be taken into account in explanations of our educational influences. I want to focus your awareness on the relational dynamic that explanatory principles will need to include.

Here is the visual data:

- Jane Renowden, *How do I create my living-educational-theories of practice?* BERA 08. http://www.youtube.com/watch?v=yND2Ra7vdhQ&feature=related
- Christine Jones describing *the award of the Inclusion Quality Mark* at the Guildhall, Bath, on 4 July 2007.
  http://www.youtube.com/watch?v=eEr6JpIchlQ
- Marie Huxtable at BERA 08 on *loving recognition, respectful connectedness and educational responsibility*.
  http://www.youtube.com/watch?v=FNJnmjHQrBY .
- Jack Whitehead presenting a *keynote at the International Conference of Teacher Research* in April 2008 in New York.
  https://youtu.be/KXLqGAAK-D0.
- Jean McNiff in 2008 sharing information on her *support for action research in global contexts* (including Khayelitsha in South Africa) with colleagues at St. Mary's College.
  http://www.youtube.com/watch?v=jsbelPVpUC8 .
- Margaret Farren (far right) with an *Action Research group at Dublin City University*.
  http://www.youtube.com/watch?v=mG1KK8VElZk

As I focus below on educational influences with educational responsibility, the meanings of practical principles, and the units, standards and logics of the new epistemology, I am asking you to bear in mind that the video clips are showing you some of the living spaces, with their diversity and ecological complexity, from which our explanations of our educational influences are emerging. I cannot overemphasise, as I explain below, the importance of comprehending the importance of a relationally dynamic awareness of space and boundaries in understanding this ecological complexity (Rayner, 2006).

2. Reasons For Focusing On Educational Influences In Learning With Educational Responsibility

I have two main reasons for choosing to focus on educational influences in learning. The first comes from my desire to acknowledge the importance of the creative responsiveness of the other, in their own learning, in what counts for me as an educational influence. The second comes from my resistance to the idea of causal determination in my educational influences in the learning of another. For me to recognise an influence as educational I need to see that, whatever I might do with another person in an educational relationship, there is a creative and critical response by the other in what they are learning from what I am doing.

I feel supported in my focus on influence by Said's (1997) use of a quotation from Valéry:

> No word comes easier or oftener to the critic's pen than the word influence, and no vaguer notion can be found among all the vague notions that compose the phantom armory of aesthetics. Yet there is nothing in the critical field that should be of greater philosophical interest or prove more rewarding to analysis than the progressive modification of one mind by the work of another (p. 15).

My choice of focus on educational responsibility comes from my sense of vocation in education. Working as an educator with my students or as an educational researcher in contributing to educational theory I accept an educational responsibility towards the other. What I mean by this responsibility in my educational relationships with my students has been influenced by the ideas of Martin Buber.

Buber says that if an educator should ever believe that for the sake of education he or she has to practise selection and arrangement, then he or she will be guided by another criterion than that of inclination, however legitimate this may be in its own sphere; he or she will be guided by the recognition of values which is in his or her glance as an educator. But, says Buber:

> … even then the selection remains suspended, under constant correction by the special humility of the educator for whom the life and particular being of all

the pupils is the decisive factor to which his or her 'hierarchical' recognition is subordinated (Buber, 1947, p. 122).

Working as an educational researcher, my sense of educational responsibility has been influenced by a decision to recognise the importance of personal knowledge. This is the decision to understand the world from my point of view, as a person claiming originality and exercising my personal judgement responsibly with universal intent (Polanyi, p. 327). I distinguish what counts as educational research from education research through the expression of an educational responsibility. I see the responsibility of researchers in disciplines of education to their discipline as distinct from my educational responsibility as an educational researcher.

The significance of placing educational responsibility at the heart of my educational research can be related to Biesta's (2006) idea that we come into the world as unique individuals through the ways in which we respond responsibly to what and who is other. Biesta argues that the responsibility of the educator not only lies in the cultivation of "worldly spaces" in which the encounter with otherness and difference is a real possibility. I agree with Biesta that this extends to asking "difficult questions": questions that summon us to respond responsively and responsibly to otherness and difference in our own, unique ways (p. ix).

My focus on explaining educational influences in learning with educational responsibility includes the assumption that we are all unique human beings. Farren (2005) has emphasised this in her research into the pedagogy of the unique. Our constellations of values and understandings help to distinguish our uniqueness. The uniqueness of our lives and learning has also been influenced by the unique constellations of historical and sociocultural contexts in which we live and work.

My purpose in sustaining my research programme into educational theory is grounded in the belief that professionalism in education will be enhanced by the recognition and academic legitimation of the unique expressions of the embodied knowledge of master and doctor educators in their living-educational-theories. I recognise the following educators, amongst others, as doctor educators because they have produced explanations for their educational influences worthy of the award of a doctoral degree.

The five doctoral degrees of primary school teachers from the Republic of Ireland, awarded by the University of Limerick were supervised by Jean McNiff. Because the role of higher education, in supporting teachers in making public and evolving their embodied knowledge as educators, is not always appreciated, it is worth stressing the significance of this support in the creation of the teachers' community of practice and knowledge-creation. The two doctoral degrees of the secondary school teachers awarded by the University of Bath were supervised by myself, and I provided similar support to Jean in making public and evolving the embodied knowledge of the doctor educators:

- *How Do I Come To Understand My Shared Living Educational Standards Of Judgement In The Life I Lead With Others? Creating The Space For Intergenerational Student-Led Research.* (2008) Karen Riding's PhD thesis (University of Bath).
- *How Do I Contribute To The Education Of Myself And Others Through Improving The Quality Of Living Educational Space? The Story Of Living Myself Through Others As A Practitioner-Researcher.* (2008) Simon Riding's PhD thesis (University of Bath).
- *Helping Eagles Fly – A Living Theory Approach to Student and Young Adult Leadership Development.* (2008) Chris Glavey's PhD thesis (University of Glamorgan).
- *Towards A Living Theory Of Caring Pedagogy: Interrogating My Practice To Nurture A Critical, Emancipatory And Just Community Of Enquiry.* (2007) Mary Roche's PhD thesis (University of Limerick).
- *A Living Theory Of A Practice Of Social Justice: Realising The Right Of Traveller Children To Educational Equality.* (2006) Bernie Sullivan's PhD thesis (University of Limerick).
- *My Living Theory Of Learning To Teach For Social Justice: How Do I Enable Primary School Children With Specific Learning Disability (Dyslexia) And Myself As Their Teacher To Realise Our Learning Potentials?* (2007) Caitriona McDonagh's PhD thesis (University of Limerick).
- *My Living Educational Theory Of Inclusional Practice.* (2007) Margaret Cahill's PhD thesis (University of Limerick).
- *Working With Collaborative Projects: My Living Theory Of A Holistic Educational Practice.* (2006) Máirín Glenn's PhD thesis (University of Limerick).

I shall now turn to the meanings of the practical principles with their energy-flowing values that can constitute explanations of educational influence. It is understanding the nature of these practical principles that contributes to establishing a new epistemology for educational knowledge with educational responsibility.

3. Meanings Of The Practical Principles That Can Constitute Explanations Of Educational Influence.

Of key significance in understanding the nature of practical principles, in explanations of educational influence, is that education is a value-laden practical activity (Peters, 1966). To explain the educational influences of these activities we need to understand the practical principles that move or guide the activities.

For example, I am moved to act in support of academic freedom when I feel that this freedom is denied. I can explain what I am doing in terms of the motivating influence of the practical principle of academic freedom. I can also explain (Whitehead, 1993) what I am doing in terms of my understandings of the historical and sociocultural influences that are working to support the negation of academic freedom and those that are working to enhance the realisation of academic freedom. In my early experiences in 1971, of feeling that a mistake was being made in the disciplines approach to educational theory, I could not clearly articulate the reasons for this mistake. I had to wait for Paul Hirst's (1983) explication of the mistake for me to be able to understand the mistake in terms of the practical principles that can explain educational influences in learning.

Hirst explained the mistake when he said that an understanding of educational theory will be developed:

> ... in the context of immediate practical experience and will be co-terminous with everyday understanding. In particular, many of its operational principles, both explicit and implicit, will be of their nature generalisations from practical experience and have as their justification the results of individual activities and practices.

> In many characterisations of educational theory, my own included, principles justified in this way have until recently been regarded as at best pragmatic maxims having a first crude and superficial justification in practice that in any rationally developed theory would be replaced by principles with more fundamental, theoretical justification. That now seems to me to be a mistake. Rationally defensible practical principles, I suggest, must of their nature stand up to such practical tests and without that are necessarily inadequate (Hirst, 1983, p. 18).

What I had experienced, in my continuing professional development at the Institute of Education, was the pressure to replace my practical principles, the energy-flowing, values-laden principles I used to make sense of what I was doing with my pupils and in my professional learning, by the principles with so-called 'more fundamental, theoretical justification'.

In contribution to the explication of a new epistemology for educational knowledge with educational responsibility I want to introduce some meanings of the energy-flowing values in the explanatory principles and in the standards of judgement that distinguish educational explanations of educational influence from other forms of explanation. The introduction uses ostensive expressions of meaning as well as lexical definitions of meaning. By the ostensive expression of meaning, I mean that, using video clips of practice, I point to where I experience an empathetic resonance with my own meanings and check the validity of my response with the other. By lexical definitions I mean that meanings of words are defined in terms of other words.

I now want to use digital technology in visual narratives to show my understanding of practical principles that can explain educational influences in learning. Using the e-version of *Research Intelligence*, Huxtable (2009a) has given a more detailed demonstration of how the use of digital technology with visual narratives can be used to communicate meanings of energy-flowing and values-laden explanatory principles.

The following video is from a talk I gave on Ubuntu at the University of the Free State, South Africa, on 28 February 2006. The digital technology allows the 3:29-minute clip to be played quickly forwards and backwards in a way that communicates the relationally dynamic nature of the event. Individuals are existing within this living educational space (Riding, 2008) as I express my understandings of the energy-flowing values of Ubuntu. At 2:42 minutes I am explicitly expressing my own life-affirming energy with values.

http://www.youtube.com/watch?v=CkKyeT0osz8.

I want to emphasise the importance of understanding the influence of communities of practice and knowledge-creation in the expression of my energy-flowing values of Ubuntu as explanatory principles. Eden Charles (2007) introduced me to the idea of Ubuntu in relation to his explanatory principles of moving beyond decolonisation with guiltless recognition and societal re-identification in his doctoral thesis. Jean McNiff organised the workshops and lectures in a visit to South Africa that enabled me to share ideas on Action Research and Living Theory research. In talking about living standards of judgement I have been influenced by the original ideas of Moira Laidlaw (1996) in her doctoral thesis. I say this to acknowledge the multiple influences in my own learning from belonging to a community of practice and knowledge-creation.

I now want to focus on the significance of such expressions of energy with values in living educational spaces in communicating meanings of practical principles. I am thinking of practical principles that acknowledge the influence of diverse cultural contexts and complex ecologies through the relationally dynamic awareness of inclusionality (Rayner, 2009). I use Rayner's understanding of inclusionality as the expression of a relationally dynamic awareness of space and boundaries as continuous, connective, reflective and co-creative.

For Rayner (2006) the key to moving into this relationally dynamic awareness lies in finding ways that enable ourselves and others to 'see through' the visual illusion that leads us mentally to isolate what we observe from what includes what we observe, including ourselves. Bateson (1987) advocated a similar move in his steps to an ecology of mind. I have integrated this insight in another publication in the development of a living-theory methodology (Whitehead, 2009).

Drawing on Jones' research I now want to present the evidence-based claim that the relationally dynamic qualities of practical principles, together with their energy-flowing values, can be recognised and communicated with the help of digital technology. The inclusion of e-media in research degrees of the University of Bath was permitted in 2004 by a change in regulation governing the submission of research degrees. Jones (2009) has used digital technology in her multimedia enquiry for her master's degree at Bath Spa University on 'How Do I Improve My Practice As An Inclusion Officer, Working In A Children's Service?'

Jones communicates her meanings of inclusion in expressing her energy-flowing educational values as she explains her educational and systemic influence in enhancing inclusion within schools in Bath and North East Somerset. The multimedia dissertation includes the clip below of an explanation of when Jones decided to become a teacher after feeling mortified by a primary teacher's response.

As Jones explains on the video clip why she decided to become a teacher I feel an empathetic resonance (Sardello, 2008) with both Jones' expression of being mortified and her passionate response to 'do it the right way'. Jones' energy-flowing value to 'do it the right way' resonates with my own expressions of a life-affirming energy and values-based desire to make appropriate educational responses with my students.

http://www.youtube.com/watch?v=jXvrgS5xjdY

I have checked with Jones that we are sharing a recognition of her expression of a life-affirming energy when she expresses her desire to 'do it the right way'. I am claiming that such flows of energy with values can be comprehended by ourselves and others as explanatory principles in our explanation of educational influence in our own learning and in the learning of others.

I will not have time during this presentation to check the validity of my interpretations of the energy-flowing values that are used by other participants in this symposium as their practical principles. However, I do have time to state my responses to the above video clips in which I draw on my experience of empathetic resonance. Making these claims public means that their validity can be tested. I am thinking of my responses to Jane Renowden in which I experience her energy-flowing value of accountability as a practical principle. I experience Margaret Farren's expression of her Celtic spirituality as a practical principle. I experience my own expression of life-affirming energy with Ubuntu as a practical principle. I experience Jean McNiff's energy-flowing value of being a global citizen as a practical principle. I experience the practical principles of Marie Huxtable's expression of loving recognition, respectful connectedness and educational responsibility.

As I communicate the meanings of the practical principles that can constitute explanations of educational influence I am aware of how much I have learned about these principles from the doctoral researchers I have worked with.

Over the past 14 years my research supervisions have included some 27 successfully completed living-theory doctoral theses, including my own. The living-theories have been generated within the influence of complex ecologies and diverse cultural settings in China, the USA, Canada, Japan, the UK, the Republic of Ireland and India. You can access these in the Living Theory section of http://www.actionresearch.net.

I include a list of these theses (Appendix 2) for you to access at your leisure from the live urls in the references. Each researcher gave great attention to their abstract. These are short enough for you to read quickly and appreciate the originality of each researcher in clarifying the meanings of the value-laden practical principles they use in their explanations of their educational influences in their own learning and in the learning of others. Each of their living-educational-theories is unique. However, I believe that as you engage with their theses you will experience, through your empathetic resonance, the meanings of energy-flowing values in their practical explanatory principles that carry hope for the future of humanity and our own.

My learning from these research programmes of these doctoral researchers, together with my learning from my own, informs my understanding below of the units of appraisal, the living standards of judgement (Laidlaw, 1996) and the living logics that can help to make explicit the new epistemology for educational knowledge with educational responsibility (Whitehead, 2009a and b).

4. The Units Of Appraisal, The Living Standards Of Judgement And The Living Logics That Help To Constitute Living-Educational-Theories With Educational Responsibility.

In an epistemology, as a theory of knowledge, it is important to understand what is being judged in terms of its validity. This is the unit of appraisal. It is important to understand how it is being judged. This refers to the standards of judgement. Logic is fundamental to an epistemology because this is the mode of thought that is appropriate for comprehending the real as rational (Marcuse, 1964, p. 105).

There has been a 2,500-year battle between logicians who advocate either propositional or dialectical logics. The battle has focused on the issue of contradiction.

In answering his question, 'What is Dialectic?', Popper (1963) rejected dialectical claims to knowledge as 'without the slightest foundation. Indeed, they are based on nothing better than a loose and woolly way of speaking' (p. 316).

Popper demonstrated, using two laws of inference, that if a theory contains a contradiction, then it entails everything, and therefore, indeed, nothing. He says that a theory which adds to every information which it asserts also the negation of this information can give us no information at all. A theory which involves a contradiction is therefore entirely useless as a theory (p. 317).

On the other hand, Marcuse (1964) claimed that propositional theories masked the dialectical nature of reality with its nucleus of contradiction. In one of the most impressive displays of understanding dialectical logic, Ilyenkov (1977, p. 313) was still left with the problem of contradiction when he asked, 'If an object exists as a living contradiction what must the thought be (statement about the object) that expresses it?' Ilyenkov did not have the benefits of digital technology that enables individuals to focus on the living logics in their lives and in the explanations of their educational influences in learning. Ilyenkov was constrained by the limitations of communicating meanings within statements on pages of printed text.

In the generation of an individual's living-educational-theory the unit of appraisal is the individual's explanation of their educational influence in learning. This can be an explanation of the individual's educational influence in their own learning, in the learning of others, and/or in the learning of social formations.

The standards of judgement are living in the sense of including energy-flowing values that contribute to the practical principles we can use to explain our educational influences. Each individual has a unique constellation of these values. They are embodied in what the individual is doing. They are influenced by the complex ecologies in which the individual lives and works. Their meanings can be clarified and evolved in the course of their emergence in practice. They are also 'living' standards of judgement (Laidlaw, 1996) in the sense that they can evolve in the course of their clarification. To prevent the living standards from becoming seen as 'discrete' entities, rather than 'distinct' relationally dynamic expressions of energy-flowing values, I emphasise the importance of visual narratives (Jones, 2009; Riding, K., 2008; Riding, S., 2008) in retaining this relationally dynamic awareness of space and boundaries (Rayner, 2006).

To fully appreciate the significance of living standards of judgement in the new epistemology for educational knowledge I think that you may need to engage with the visual narratives of living theorists such as Naidoo (2005), Farren (2005) and Charles (2007). They use video clips of themselves to communicate the meanings of their embodied, energy-flowing values in their living standards of judgement. Naidoo uses video to communicate the meanings of a passion for compassion. Farren uses video to communicate her meanings of a web of betweenness with her Celtic spirituality and pedagogy of the unique. Charles uses video to communicate the explicit meanings of living Ubuntu as a standard of judgement in an explanation of moving beyond postcolonialism through guiltless recognition and societal re-identification. Ubuntu originated in Africa and is a way of being that recognises 'I am because we are'.

Each individual lives with a unique constellation of embodied values that they can clarify and communicate to others as the living standards of judgement they use in their living-theories. In these theories the individual both holds themselves to account for living their values as fully as they can and evaluates the validity of their knowledge-claims in their living-educational-theories. One of the significant contributions a community of practice can make to the knowledge-creation is in enhancing the validity of the researchers' explanations. This can be done my members of the community of practice acting as a validation group through asking questions derived from Habermas' (1976) four criteria of social validity, such as:

1. How could comprehensibility be improved?
2. Is there sufficient evidence to justify the assertions?
3. Is there an awareness of the normalising influence of the historical and sociocultural context?
4. Does the account provide evidence of a sustained commitment, over time and interaction, of a desire to live values and evolve understandings as fully as possible?

The idea of a living logic is fundamental in explicating the new epistemology for educational knowledge. Living logics, in the sense of modes of thinking that are appropriate for comprehending the real as rational, can be understood with the help of visual narratives in the generation of living-educational-theories. The explanations of educational influence of self-study researchers are rarely, if ever, smooth stories of self. They contain some narrative wreckage and the creative and improvisatory responses of individuals to difficult experiences. In criticising Popper's logic of scientific discovery, the Nobel Prize-winner Medawar (1969) explained that:

> The major defect of the hypothetico-deductive scheme, considered as a formulary of scientific behaviour, is its disavowal of any competence to speak about the generative act in scientific enquiry, 'having an idea,' for this represents the imaginative or logically unscripted episode in scientific thinking, the part that lies outside logic. The objection is all the more grave because an imaginative or inspirational process enters into all scientific reasoning at every level: it is not confined to 'great' discoveries, as the more simple-minded inductivists have supposed (p. 55).

For Medawar the purpose of scientific enquiry is not to compile an inventory of factual information, nor to build up a totalitarian world picture of natural laws in which every event that is not compulsory is forbidden. He says that we should think of it rather:

> ... as a logically articulated structure of justifiable beliefs about nature. It begins as a story about a Possible World – a story which we invent and criticize and modify as we go along, so that it ends by being, as nearly as we can make it, a story about real life (Medawar, 1969, p. 59).

Through generating and sharing our living-educational-theories (Whitehead, 2009b) that offer valid explanations of influences in real life, I believe that educational researchers are contributing to enhancing the flows of energy and values that carry hope for the future of humanity. I think that it is worth repeating that I am hoping that you are persuaded of the validity of the new epistemology and that making such contributions to education constitutes a worthwhile form of life.

There are several ways in which we could continue an educational conversation on the issues raised in this symposium. We could make responses to the Open Dialogue contributions in *Research Intelligence*, by Bruce Ferguson (2008); Whitehead (2008a and b); Adler-Collins (2008); Laidlaw (2008); and Huxtable (2009a). If you are not already a participant you could join the 2009–2010 practitioner-researcher conversation in the JISC Forum at:

https://www.jiscmail.ac.uk/cgi-bin/webadmin?SUBED1=practitioner-researcher&A=1.

We could help each other over the coming year to enhance our educational influences in our practice, to generate educational knowledge and to submit proposals on our contributions to educational knowledge for BERA 2010. I do hope that we find a way to continue to share our ideas and to extend our educational influences over the coming year and beyond. Through extending, deepening and communicating our knowledge-creation in our communities of practice I believe that we will enhance professionalism in education in both our local and global contexts. This belief is evidence-based, as I hope that I have just shown and shared in my learning from the 36-year educational research programme at the University of Bath. I value highly the opportunities provided by BERA annual conferences and this keynote symposium in particular, for sharing and evaluating the validity of these ideas on explicating a new educational epistemology for educational knowledge with educational responsibility.

Last Saturday on 29 August 2009 – my 65th birthday – I received an unexpected gift that has relevance for this presentation. Robyn Pound (2003), a health visitor and friend, whose doctoral research programme on alongsideness at the University of the West of England I responded to, brought round a book with the title Jack Whitehead Validations (Pound, Laidlaw and Huxtable, 2009). This beautifully bound book contained some 57 contributions from individuals who had responded to a letter from Robyn Pound and Moira Laidlaw that included the suggestion:

.... We suggest a short piece of not more than 100 words explaining what Jack and Living Theory means to you.

The contributions communicate affirmations of the energy and values that distinguish my pedagogy and ideas. Collectively they provide a most impressive public validation of my belief in the significance of creating and sharing our living-educational-theories as explanations of our educational influences in our own learning, in the learning of others and in the learning of social formations. I am thinking of the significance in terms of living a loving and productive life whilst engaged in ontological enquiries of the kind, 'How can I enhance a meaningful life in the world with others?' and in practical questions of the kind, 'How do I improve what I am doing?'

Jack Whitehead Validations (Pound, Laidlaw and Huxtable can be downloaded from http://www.actionresearch.net/writings/jack/validationsoneopt.pdf

APPENDIX 1

Background to the research

There has been much discussion in BERA and AERA about the appropriate standards of judgement for evaluating the quality and validity of the educational knowledge generated by practitioner-researchers.

The 1988 BERA Presidential Address focused on the development of a research-based approach to professionalism in education through the generation of living-educational-theories. By 2008 over 30 living-theory doctorates had been legitimated in the Academy with new units of appraisal, living logics and standards of judgement, in explanations of educational influences in learning.

The research answers the calls made by Schön (1995) for the development of a new epistemology for the scholarship of teaching, and by Snow (2001) to develop methodologies for making public the professional knowledge of teachers.

Foci of the enquiries

There are three research questions addressed in this presentation:

1. Can the explanations produced by individuals to explain their educational influences in learning be used as appropriate units of appraisal in the generation of educational theory?
2. What are the logics of the explanations that individuals produce for their educational influences in their own learning?
3. Which living standards of judgement for evaluating the validity of explanations of educational influences in learning have been legitimated in the Academy?

Research methods

The appropriateness of the action-reflection cycles used in the generation and development of living-educational-theories rests in showing their usefulness in clarifying the meanings of ontological values in educational relationships and in forming these values into living epistemological standards of judgement.

Visual narratives are used in multimedia explanations of educational influences in learning.

The methods for enhancing the robustness of the validity and rigour of the explanations include the use of Habermas' (1976) four criteria of social validity and Winter's (1989) six criteria for enhancing rigour.

Lather's (1991) catalytic validity is used to justify claims about the educational influence of the ideas generated in one context for individuals working and researching in different contexts in the UK, Ireland, Canada, Croatia, India, China, Japan and South Africa.

Theoretical frameworks

Answers to the research questions include the following analytic frames:

Adler-Collins' (2000) safe space; Bernstein's (2000) mythological discourse; Biesta's (2006) language of education; Bourdieu's (2000) ideas of habitus and social formation; Charles' (2007) guiltless recognition and societal re-identification; Delong's (2002) culture of enquiry; Farren's (2005) pedagogy of the unique and web of betweenness; Habermas' (1976, 1987, 2002) notions of social validity, learning and the inclusion of the other; Hymer's (2007) idea of giftedness; Ilyenkov's (1977) dialectical logic; Lohr's (2006) love at work; McNiff's (2006) my story is my living-educational-theory; Merleau-Ponty's (1972) notion of embodiment; Rayner's (2006) idea of inclusionality; Vasilyuk's (1996) psychology of experiencing; Whitehead's (1989) idea of living-educational-theories; Laidlaw's (1996) idea of living standards of judgement; and Winter's (1989) criteria of rigour.

Contribution to new educational knowledge

1. The generation of a new epistemology for educational knowledge (Whitehead, 2008 a and b).
2. The explication of a living-theory methodology for making public the embodied knowledge of professional practitioners.
3. An understanding of educational theory as the explanations that individuals produce for their educational influences in learning.

References (including the references for Whitehead's paper)

Adler-Collins, J. (2000) A Scholarship Of Enquiry. MA dissertation, University of Bath.

Adler-Collins, J.P. (2008) Creating New Forms Of Living Educational Theories Through Collaborative Educational Research From Eastern And Western Contexts: A response to Jack Whitehead. *Research Intelligence,* 104; 17–18.

Bateson, G. (1987) *Steps to an ecology of mind.* London: Jason Aronson.

Bernstein, B. (2000) *Pedagogy, Symbolic Control and Identity: Theory, Research, Critique.* Lanham, Boulder, New York, Oxford: Rowman & Littlefield.

Bourdieu, P. (1990) *The Logic of Practice.* Stanford, CA: Stanford University Press.

Biesta, G.J.J. (2006) *Beyond Learning: Democratic Education for a Human Future.* Boulder: Paradigm Publishers.

Bruce Ferguson, P. (2008) Increasing Inclusion in Educational Research: Reflections from New Zealand. *Research Intelligence,* 102; 24–25.

Buber, M. (1947) *Between Man & Man.* London: Kegan Paul, Trench, Trubner & Co.

Charles, E. (2007) *How Do I Improve My Practice? Creating A Decolonising Living Educational Theory That Embraces And Extends Our Humanity Into New Relationships That Carry Hope For Humanity*. PhD thesis, University of Bath.

Delong, J. (2002) *How Can I Improve My Practice As A Superintendent Of Schools And Create My Own Living Educational Theory?* PhD thesis, University of Bath.

Farren, M. (2005) *Creating My Pedagogy Of The Unique Through A Web Of Betweenness*. PhD thesis, University of Bath.

Farren, M. (2009) *Action Research: Living Theory Collaboratory*. Retrieved on the 23 August 2009 from http://83.70.181.166/joomlamgt/index.php?option=com_content&view=article &id=166&Itemid=62 (no longer live).

Habermas, J. (2002) *The Inclusion of the Other: Studies in Political Theory*. Oxford: Polity.

Habermas, J. (1987) *The Theory of Communicative Action, Volume Two: The Critique of Functionalist Reason*. Oxford: Polity.

Habermas, J. (1976) *Communication and the Evolution of Society*. London: Heinemann.

Hirst, P. (Ed.) (1983) *Educational Theory and Its Foundation Disciplines*. London: Routledge and Kegan Paul.

Huxtable, M. (2009a) How do we contribute to an educational knowledge base? A response to Whitehead and a challenge to BERJ. *Research Intelligence*, 107; 25–26.

Huxtable, M. (2009b) *How Do I Improve What I Am Doing In My Professional Practice And Make An Original Contribution To The Knowledge Base Of Education?* A contribution to BERA 2009 annual conference keynote symposium on 'Explicating A New Epistemology For Educational Knowledge With Educational Responsibility' on 3 September 2009 at the University of Manchester. Retrieved 30 August from http://www.actionresearch.net/writings/bera09/mhberasymsept09.pdf.

Hymer, B. (2007) *How Do I Understand And Communicate My Values And Beliefs In My Work As An Educator In The Field Of Giftedness?* D. Ed. Psy. thesis, Newcastle University.

Ilyenkov, E. (1977) *Dialectical Logic*. Moscow: Progress Publishers.

Jones, C. (2009) How Do I Improve My Practice And An Inclusion Officer Working In A Children's Service. MA dissertation Bath Spa University. Retrieved 21 July 2009 from http://www.actionresearch.net/living/cjmaok/cjma.htm.

Laidlaw, M. (1996) *How Can I Create My Own Living Educational Theory As I Offer You An Account Of My Own Educational Development?* PhD thesis, University of Bath. Retrieved 22 July 2009 from http://www.actionresearch.net/living/moira2.shtml

Laidlaw, M. (2008) Increasing Inclusion in Educational Research: A Response to Pip Bruce Ferguson and Jack Whitehead. *Research Intelligence*, 104; 16–17.

Lather, P. (1991). *Getting Smart: Feminist Research and Pedagogy With/In the Postmodern*. New York: Routledge.

Lee, C.D. and Rochon, R. (2009) *2010 AERA Annual Meeting Theme: Understanding Complex Ecologies in a Changing World*. Retrieved 22 July 2009 from http://www.aera.net/Events-Meetings/Annual-Meeting/Previous-Annual-Meetings/2010-Annual-Meeting.

Lohr, E. (2006) *What Is My Lived Experience Of Love And How May I Become An Instrument Of Love's Purpose*. PhD thesis, University of Bath.

McNiff, J. (2006) My Story Is My Living Educational Theory, in Clandinin, J. (Ed.) *Handbook of Narrative Inquiry*. London; New York: Sage.

McNiff, J. (2009) *Learning For Action In Action*. A paper for the Keynote Symposium of the British Educational Research Association on 'Explicating A New Epistemology For Educational Knowledge With Educational Responsibility, at the University of Manchester, 3 September 2009. Retrieved 30 August 2009 from http://www.jeanmcniff.com/userfiles/file/Publications/Bera09/JMBERA09Keynote.pdf.

Medawar, P. (1969) *Induction and Intuition in Scientific Thought.* London: Methuen & Co.

Merleau-Ponty, M. (1972) *Phenomenology of Perception.* London: Routledge.

Naidoo, M. (2005) *I Am Because We Are (A Never Ending Story). The Emergence Of A Living Theory Of Inclusional And Responsive Practice.* PhD thesis, University of Bath. Retrieved 21 July 2009 from http://www.actionresearch.net/naidoo.shtml .

Peters, R.S. (1966) *Ethics and Education.* London: Allen & Unwin.

Polanyi, M. (1958) *Personal Knowledge: Towards a Post-Critical Philosophy.* London: Routledge and Kegan Paul.

Popper, K. (1963) *Conjectures and Refutations.* Oxford: Oxford University Press.

Pound, R. (2003) *How Can I Improve My Health Visiting Support Of Parenting? The Creation Of An Alongside Epistemology Through Action Enquiry.* PhD thesis, University of the West of England. Retrieved 30 August 2009 from http://www.actionresearch.net/pound.shtml.

Pound, R., Laidlaw, M. and Huxtable, M. (Eds.) (2009) *Jack Whitehead Validations.* Bath: Bear Flat Publishing. Retrieved 30 August 2009 from http://www.actionresearch.net/jackvalidations.htm.

Rayner, A. (2009) *What is Inclusionality.* Retrieved 12 July 2009 from http://www.inclusionality.org/index.php?option=com_content&view=article&id =1&Itemid=2 (no longer available).

Rayner, A. (2006) *Essays And Talks About 'Inclusionality' by Alan Rayner.* Retrieved 11 January 2008 from http://people.bath.ac.uk/bssadmr/inclusionality (no longer available).

Renowden, J. (2009) *Linking Accountability With Professional Identity: How Do I Develop My Living Theory Of Educationally Responsible Practice?* A presentation in the keynote symposium on Explicating A New Epistemology For Educational Knowledge With Educational Responsibility at the 2009 BERA Annual Conference in the University of Manchester. Retrieved on 30 August 2009 from http://www.jackwhitehead.com/bera09keysym/janerBERA09dr220809.pdf.

Riding, K. (2008) *How Do I Come To Understand My Shared Living Educational Standards Of Judgement In The Life I Lead With Others? Creating The Space For Intergenerational Student-Led Research.* PhD thesis, University of Bath. Retrieved 21 July 2009 from http://www.actionresearch.net/karenridingphd.shtml .

Riding, S. (2008) *How Do I Contribute To The Education Of Myself And Others Through Improving The Quality Of Living Educational Space? The Story Of Living Myself Through Others As A Practitioner-Researcher.* PhD thesis, University of Bath. Retrieved 21 July 2009 from http://www.actionresearch.net/simonridingphd.shtml .

Said, E.W. (1997) *Beginnings: Intention and Method.* p. 15. London: Granta.

Sardello, R. (2008) *Silence: The Mystery of Wholeness.* Berkeley: Goldenstone Press.

Vasilyuk, F. (1991) *The Psychology of Experiencing: The Resolution of Life's Critical Situations.* Hemel Hempstead: Harvester Wheatsheaf.

Whitehead, J. (1989) Creating A Living Educational Theory From Questions Of The Kind, 'How Do I Improve My Practice?' *Cambridge Journal of Education,* 19(1); 41–52.

Whitehead, J. (1993) *The Growth of Educational Knowledge: Creating Your Own Living*

Educational Theories. Bournemouth: Hyde. Retrieved 17 March 2018 from
http://www.actionresearch.net/writings/jwgek93.htm

Whitehead, J. (2006) Living Inclusional Values In Educational Standards Of Practice And Judgement, *Ontario Action Researcher*, Vol. 8.2.1. Retrieved 12 January 2007 from http://oar.nipissingu.ca/PDFS/V821E.pdf.

Whitehead, J. (2008a) Increasing Inclusion In Educational Research: A Response To Pip Bruce Ferguson. *Research Intelligence*, 103; 16–17.

Whitehead, J. (2008b) An Epistemological Transformation in what counts as Educational Knowledge: Responses to Laidlaw and Adler-Collins. *Research Intelligence*, 105; 28–29.

Whitehead, J. (2009a) How Do I Influence the Generation of Living Educational Theories for Personal and Social Accountability in Improving Practice? Using a Living Theory Methodology in Improving Educational Practice, pp. 173–194 in Tidwell, Deborah L.; Heston, Melissa L.; Fitzgerald, Linda M. (Eds.) (2009) *Research Methods for the Self-Study of Practice*. Dordrecht: Springer.

Whitehead, J. (2009b) Generating Living Theory And Understanding In Action Research Studies. *Action Research*, 7 (1); 85–99.

Whitehead, J. (2009c) *Generating Educational Theories That Can Explain Educational Influences In Learning*. A presentation in the keynote symposium on Explicating A New Epistemology For Educational Knowledge With Educational Responsibility at the 2009 BERA Annual Conference in the University of Manchester. Retrieved on 30 August 2009 from http://www.jackwhitehead.com/bera09keysym/jwbera09paper230809opt.pdf.

Whitehead, J. and McNiff, J. (2006) *Action Research Living Theory*. London: Sage.

Winter, R. (1989) *Learning from Experience*. London: Falmer.

APPENDIX 2

List and Access to Doctoral Theses

(Note – Holley's M.Phil dissertation has been included because of its focus on living theory. The theses of Hymer and Rawal are included for the same reason and were awarded by the universities of Newcastle and Worcester, respectively.)

Karen Riding's PhD (2008) thesis, *How Do I Come To Understand My Shared Living Educational Standards Of Judgement In The Life I Lead With Others? Creating The Space For Intergenerational Student-Led Research.* Retrieved 11 March 2009 from http://www.actionresearch.net/karenridingphd.shtml.

Simon Riding's PhD (2008) thesis, *How Do I Contribute To The Education Of Myself And Others Through Improving The Quality Of Living Educational Space? The Story Of Living Myself Through Others As A Practitioner-Researcher.* Retrieved 11 March 2009 from http://www.actionresearch.net/simonridingphd.shtml.

Jocelyn Jones' PhD (2008) thesis, *Thinking With Stories Of Suffering: Towards A Living Theory Of Response-Ability.* Retrieved 11 March 2009 from http://www.actionresearch.net/jocelynjonesphd.shtml.

Joan Walton's PhD (2008) thesis, *Ways Of Knowing: Can I Find A Way Of Knowing That Satisfies My Search For Meaning?* Retrieved 11 March 2009 from http://www.actionresearch.net/walton.shtml (no longer available).

Jane Spiro's PhD (2008) thesis, How I Have Arrived At A Notion Of Knowledge Transformation, Through Understanding The Story Of Myself As Creative Writer, Creative Educator, Creative Manager, And Educational Researcher. Graduated 25 June 2008, University of Bath. Retrieved 11 March 2009 from http://www.actionresearch.net/janespirophd.shtml.

Je Kan Adler-Collins' PhD (2007) thesis, Developing An Inclusional Pedagogy Of The Unique: How Do I Clarify, Live And Explain My Educational Influences In My Learning As I Pedagogise My Healing Nurse Curriculum In A Japanese University? Graduated 25 June 2008, University of Bath. Retrieved 11 March 2009 from http://www.actionresearch.net/jekan.shtml.

Eden Charles' PhD (2007) thesis, How Can I bring Ubuntu As A Living Standard Of Judgment Into The Academy? Moving Beyond Decolonisation Through Societal Reidentification And Guiltless Recognition. Retrieved 11 March 2009 from http://www.actionresearch.net/edenphd.shtml .

Eleanor Lohr's PhD (2006) thesis, Love At Work: What Is My Lived Experience Of Love, And How May I Become An Instrument Of Love's Purpose? Retrieved 11 March 2009 from http://www.actionresearch.net/lohr.shtml.

Margaret Farren's PhD (2005) thesis, How Can I Create A Pedagogy Of The Unique Through A Web Of Betweenness? Retrieved 11 March 2009 from http://www.actionresearch.net/farren.shtml.

Marian Naidoo's PhD (2005) thesis, I Am Because We Are (A Never Ending Story). The Emergence Of A Living Theory Of Inclusional And Responsive Practice. Retrieved 11 March 2009 from http://www.actionresearch.net/naidoo.shtml.

Madeline Church's PhD (2004) thesis, Creating An Uncompromised Place To Belong: Why Do I Find Myself In Networks? Retrieved 11 March 2009 from http://www.actionresearch.net/church.shtml.

Mary Hartog's PhD (2004) thesis, A Self Study Of A Higher Education Tutor: How Can I Improve My Practice? Retrieved 11 March 2009 from http://www.actionresearch.net/hartog.shtml.

Ram Punia's Ed.D. thesis (2004) thesis, *My CV is My Curriculum: The Making of an International Educator with Spiritual Values*. Retrieved 11 March 2009 from http://www.actionresearch.net/punia.shtml.

Paul Robert's PhD (2003) thesis, Emerging Selves In Practice: How Do I And Others Create My Practice And How Does My Practice Shape Me And Influence Others? Retrieved 11 March 2009 from http://www.actionresearch.net/roberts.shtml.

Jackie Delong's PhD (2002) thesis, *How Can I Improve My Practice As A Superintendent of Schools and Create My Own Living Educational Theory.* Retrieved 11 March 2009 from http://www.actionresearch.net/delong.shtml.

Jacqui Scholes-Rhodes' PhD (2002) thesis, From The Inside Out: Learning To Presence My Aesthetic And Spiritual Being Through The Emergent Form Of A Creative Art Of Enquiry. Retrieved 11 March 2009 from http://www.actionresearch.net/rhodes.shtml.

Mike Bosher's PhD (2001) thesis, How Can I As An Educator And Professional Development Manager Working With Teachers, Support And Enhance The Learning And Achievement Of Pupils In A Whole School Improvement Process? Retrieved 11 March 2009 from http://www.actionresearch.net/bosher.shtml.

Geoff Mead's PhD (2001) thesis, Unlatching The Gate: Realising My Scholarship Of Living Inquiry. Retrieved 11 March 2009 from http://www.actionresearch.net/mead.shtml.

James Finnegan's PhD (2000) thesis, How Do I Create My Own Educational Theory In My Educative Relations As An Action Researcher And As A Teacher? Retrieved 11 March 2009 from http://www.actionresearch.net/fin.shtml.

Terry Austin's PhD (2000) thesis, Treasures In The Snow: What Do I Know And How Do I Know It Through My Educational Enquiry Into My Practice Of Community? Retrieved 11 March 2009 from http://www.actionresearch.net/austin.shtml.

Jack Whitehead's PhD (1999) thesis, How Do I Improve My Practice? Creating A Discipline Of Education Through Educational Enquiry. Retrieved 11 March 2009 from http://www.actionresearch.net/jack.shtml.

Ben Cunningham's PhD (1999) thesis, How Do I Come To Know My Spirituality As I Create My Own Living-Educational-Theory? Retrieved 11 March 2009 from http://www.actionresearch.net/ben.shtml.

John Loftus' PhD (1999) thesis, An Action Research Enquiry Into The Marketing Of An Established First School In Its Transition To Full Primary Status. Joint supervision with Pamela Lomax at Kingston University. Retrieved 11 March 2009 from http://www.actionresearch.net/loftus.shtml.

Pat D'Arcy's PhD (1998) thesis, The Whole Story... Retrieved 11 March 2009 from http://www.actionresearch.net/pat.shtml.

Erica Holley's M.Phil. (1997) thesis, How Do I As A Teacher-Researcher Contribute To The Development Of A Living-Educational-Theory Through An Exploration Of My Values In My Professional Practice? Retrieved 11 March 2009 from http://www.actionresearch.net/erica.shtml.

Moira Laidlaw's PhD (1996) thesis, How Can I Create My Own Living-Educational-Theory As I Offer You An Account Of My Educational Development? Retrieved 11 March 2009 from http://www.actionresearch.net/moira2.shtml.

Kevin Eames' PhD (1995) thesis, How Do I, As A Teacher And Educational Action-Researcher, Describe And Explain The Nature Of My Professional Knowledge? Retrieved 11 March 2009 from http://www.actionresearch.net/kevin.shtml.

Moyra Evans' PhD (1995) thesis, An Action Research Enquiry Into Reflection In Action As Part Of My Role As A Deputy Head Teacher. Joint supervision with Pamela Lomax at Kingston University. Retrieved 11 March 2009 from http://www.actionresearch.net/moyra.shtml.

Barry Hymer's D.Ed.Psy. (2007) thesis, How Do I Understand And Communicate My Values And Beliefs In My Work As An Educator In The Field Of Giftedness? Graduated from Newcastle University, 13 July 2007. Retrieved 11 March 2009 from http://www.actionresearch.net/hymer.shtml.

Swaroop Rawal's PhD (2006) thesis, The Role Of Drama In Enhancing Life Skills In Children With Specific Learning Difficulties In A Mumbai School: My Reflective Account. Graduated from Coventry University in collaboration with the University of Worcester. Retrieved 11 March 2009 from http://www.actionresearch.net/rawal.shtml.

PAPER SIX.

Whitehead, J. (2013) *A Living Logic for Educational Research*. Presented at the 2013 Annual Conference of the British Educational Research Association, University of Sussex, 5 September.

This paper focuses on the living logic in the second component of Living Theory research in the explanations of educational influences in the learning of others. I think that it is worth repeating that the importance of logic is that it distinguishes the rationality of an explanation. I continue to follow Marcuse's (1964, p. 105) point that logic is the mode of thought that is appropriate for comprehending the real as rational. In comprehending the importance of living-logic for educational research it is worth recalling the arguments between formal and dialectical logicians about the nature of reality:

> In the classical logic, the judgement which constituted the original core of dialectical thought was formalized in the propositional form, 'S is p.' But this form conceals rather than reveals the basic dialectical proposition, which states the negative character of the empirical reality (Marcuse, 1964, p. 111).

The living logics of the explanations in the paper below include the enacting of educational reflexivity in educational relationships. Reflexivity is distinguished from reflection by adding to reflection an awareness of the principles that are structuring the reflection in generating the explanation of educational influences in learning. The nature of this reflexivity is the focus of Paper Six.

Reference

Marcuse, H. (1964) One Dimensional Man. London: Routledge and Kegan Paul.

PAPER SIX.

A Living Logic for Educational Research

A 41:31-minute video of the presentation at

http://www.youtube.com/watch?v=l4xlg3E5Vt0.

Notes to support the presentation

Abstract

For over 2,500 years there have been disputes between adherents to formal and dialectical logics about the nature of rationality. The nature of the disputes, as illustrated by Popper (1963, p. 313) and Marcuse (1964, p. 111) often focused on the problem of contradiction, where dialecticians insisted that contradiction formed the nucleus of correct thought, and formal logicians followed Aristotle in claiming that theories that contained contradictions were entirely useless as theories.

A living logic is presented, from successfully completed doctoral, educational research programmes, with a relationally dynamic form of rationality that includes 'I' as a living contradiction to dialectical logic and draws insights from propositional theories that are structured with formal logic.

Introduction

In presenting this paper at BERA 2013 on a living logic for educational research, to a session of the Special Interest Group of the Philosophy of Education, my interest in your responses goes back to my learning on the Academic Diploma course in the Philosophy of Education at the Institute of Education of the University of London between 1968 and 1970. This course was explicitly committed to the disciplines approach to educational theory in which the theory was constituted by the philosophy, psychology, sociology and history of education. I accepted this view of educational theory, passed the course and moved on to a master's degree in the psychology of education. This was completed in 1972 at the time I worked full-time as a Head of a Science Department in a London comprehensive school with a sense of vocation that focused on helping adolescents to develop their scientific understanding. This sense of vocation was reflected in my master's dissertation on 'A preliminary investigation of the process through which adolescents acquire scientific understanding' (Whitehead, 1972).

During the 1971–72 academic year I began to feel that the disciplines approach to educational theory was mistaken. This feeling was based in my experience of trying to explain my educational influences in my pupils' learning using the disciplines of education. I discovered that no discipline of education either individually or in any combination could produce a valid explanation for my educational influence in my own learning, or in the learning of my pupils. This feeling, that the dominant view of educational theory supported by philosophers of education at the country's most influential London Institute of Education was mistaken moved my sense of vocation in education to change and to seek a university post that might enable me to contribute to the creation of a valid form of educational theory. I was fortunate to be appointed as a Lecturer in Education at the University of Bath in 1973 where I could focus on making this contribution between 1973 to the end of my tenured contract in 2009 and to finishing my doctoral supervisions as a visiting research fellow in 2012.

In 1983 Paul Hirst provided me with a clear understanding of the following mistake in the disciplines approach to educational theory when he wrote that much understanding of educational theory will be developed:

> ... in the context of immediate practical experience and will be co-terminous with everyday understanding. In particular, many of its operational principles, both explicit and implicit, will be of their nature generalisations from practical experience and have as their justification the results of individual activities and practices. In many characterisations of educational theory, my own included, principles justified in this way have until recently been regarded as at best pragmatic maxims having a first crude and superficial justification in practice that in any rationally developed theory would be replaced by principles with more fundamental, theoretical justification. That now seems to me to be a mistake. Rationally defensible practical principles, I suggest, must of their nature stand up to such practical tests and without that are necessarily inadequate (Hirst, 1983, p. 18).

Part of my desire to contribute to a valid form of educational theory contained the intuitive recognition of the mistake of replacing the practical principles used by practitioners to explain their educational influence, by principles with 'more theoretical' justification.

In offering a living logic for educational research that respects such practical principles, as these are clarified in the course of their emergence in practice, I am making the following distinction between education research and educational research. I take education research to be research conducted within the conceptual frameworks and methods of validation of forms and fields of education knowledge such the philosophy, psychology, history, sociology, economic, theology, politics, economics, administration, policy and leadership of education. I take educational research to be research that produces valid explanations for the educational influences of individuals in their own learning, in the learning of others and in the learning of the social formations in which the individuals, live, work and research. In making this distinction I disagree with Whitty's point in his 2005 Presidential Address to BERA that 'educational research' is the narrower field of work specifically geared to improvement of policy and practice:

> One way of handling the distinction might be to use the terms 'education research' and 'educational research' more carefully. In this paper, I have so far used the broad term education research to characterise the whole field, but it may be that within that field we should reserve the term educational research for work that is consciously geared towards improving policy and practice..... One problem with this distinction between 'education research' as the broad term and 'educational research' as the narrower field of work specifically geared to the improvement of policy and practice is that it would mean that BERA, as the British Educational Research Association would have to change its name or be seen as only involved with the latter. So trying to make the distinction clearer would also involve BERA in a re-branding exercise which may not necessarily be the best way of spending our time and resources. But it is at least worth considering. (Whitty, 2005, p. 172–173).

I shall focus below on educational researchers as knowledge-creators in their theory creation and testing.

What follows, with its focus on a living logic for educational researchers, is a summary of my educational research programme from 1970 to 2013 as I continue to seek to make a contribution to valid forms of educational theory. The clarification and communication of this living logic rest on the growth of my educational knowledge in the enquiry, 'How do I improve what I am doing in my professional practice?' This growth is focused on the explanations I have produced in my research programme for my educational influence in my own learning, in the learning of others and in the learning of the social formations in which I live, work and research. My living logic has emerged from transformations in these explanations.

The transformations in logic described below include the transformation from the use of propositional logic, to structure the explanations in my master's dissertation on a preliminary investigation of the growth of scientific understanding in adolescents (Whitehead, 1972) to the dialectical logic that structured my doctoral thesis, *How do I improve my practice? Creating a discipline of education through educational enquiry* (Whitehead, 1999), to the living logic that structures my explanations of my educational influences in my own learning, in the learning of others and in the learning of the social formations in which I live, work and research (Whitehead, 2008).

During the course of my research programme I coined the term 'living-educational-theory' as an individual's explanation of their educational influence in their own learning in the learning of others and in the learning of the social formations in which the individual lives, works and researches. The idea of a 'living' educational theory emerged as a response to Ilyenkov's (1977, p. 313) question in his text on *Dialectical Logic*: 'If an object exists as a living contradiction what must the thought (statement about the object) be that expresses it?' One of the problems faced by dialecticians such as Ilyenkov was that they were constrained by limitations in print-based texts to write about dialectics using a medium most suited for propositional communications that abided by the law of contradictions. Until the use of multimedia digital technology for communicating embodied expressions of meaning, dialecticians, using the print-based texts of international journals, were constrained to communicating within the propositional logic that denied their rationality with their acceptance of contradiction as the nucleus of dialectics.

Multimedia accounts, especially those including digitalised visual data as evidence in explanations of educational influence, play an important role below in clarifying the nature of a living logic for educational research from explanations of educational influence. In 1972 the Inspectorate in Barking provided me with the video camera and asked me to explore its educational potential in the Science Department at Erkenwald Comprehensive School. I turned the camera on myself and was most embarrassed in experiencing myself as a living contradiction as I saw what I was doing in a classroom. I believed that I had established enquiry learning with my pupils in the sense that I was eliciting questions from my pupils and responding to them. The video showed that I was actually giving the pupils the questions, rather than helping them to form their own. This experience highlighted for me the value of visual data on my own practice in checking the validity of my beliefs about what I was doing. The inclusion of 'I' as a living contradiction in my enquiry, 'How do I improve what I am doing?' marked a transformation in my epistemology from that of a positivist scientist into the dialectical epistemology of my doctoral thesis.

The transformation of my logics continued into the living logic of my living-theory methodology (Whitehead, 2008) again with the help of visual data. At the heart of this living logic is a relationally dynamic awareness of space and boundaries (Rayner, 2005). Here is a 19-second, speeded-up video of a workshop

I am leading at the Guildhall in Bath that helped me to appreciate the importance of seeing myself with the help of such visual data in the relational dynamic of space and boundaries that my binocular vision cannot 'see directly'.

19-seconds http://www.youtube.com/watch?v=PH6DiBaZm_Y

This visual data extends my binocular perception with a view of myself in multiple dynamic relations in space. My explanations of my educational influences in my own learning and in the learning of others, as well as the social formations in which I live, work and research, have been transformed through including such visual data as evidence in showing and explaining educational responses to experiencing myself as a 'living contradiction' that exists and responds within the relationally dynamic influences of the sociohistorical and sociocultural contexts in which I live, work and research.

I first outlined the transformation in my logics from propositional to dialectical to a living logic in the 2008 multimedia account of 'Using a living-theory methodology in improving practice and generating educational knowledge in living-theories' (Whitehead, 2008). My understanding of my living logic evolved from my educational enquiry, 'How do I improve what I am doing?', into my explanation of my educational influences in learning, and then into an understanding of the logic of the explanation. In my understanding of logic I continue to use Marcuse's (1964, p. 105) idea that logic is the mode of thought that is appropriate for comprehending the real as rational.

The approach outlined below is focused on a living-theory methodology for improving practice and generating knowledge from questions of the kind, 'How do I improve what I am doing?' It also includes a new epistemology for educational knowledge. The new epistemology rests on a living logic of educational enquiry and living standards of judgement (Laidlaw, 1996) that include flows of life-affirming energy with values that carry hope for the future of humanity. The presentation emphasises the importance of the uniqueness of each individual's living-educational-theory (Whitehead, 1989) in improving practice and generating knowledge. It emphasises the importance of individual creativity in contributing to improving practice and knowledge from within historical and cultural opportunities and constraints in the social contexts of the individual's life and work. The web-based version of this presentation demonstrates the importance of local, national and international communicative collaborations for improving practice and generating knowledge in the context of globalising communications. Through its multimedia representations of educational relationships and explanations of educational influence in learning it seeks to communicate new living standards of judgement. These standards are relationally dynamic and grounded in both improving practice and generating knowledge. They express the life-affirming energy of individuals, cultures and the cosmos, with values and understandings that, it is claimed, carry hope for the future of humanity (Whitehead, 2008, p. 103).

In video 4 I include in the 2008 account in an explanation of my educational influence in the learning of social formation as I engage with institutional power relations. The explanation includes energy-flowing values as explanatory principles and in living standards of judgement.

In 1990, based on this judgement about my activities and writings, as evidence of a prima facie breach of my academic freedom, Senate established a working party on a matter of academic freedom. They reported in 1991: "The working party did not find that... his academic freedom had actually been breached. This was however, because of Mr. Whitehead's persistence in the face of pressure; a less determined individual might well have been discouraged and therefore constrained."

Video 4. Responding to matters of power and academic freedom – 57-second video at https://www.youtube.com/watch?v=MBTLfyjkFh0.

Here is my re-enactment of a meeting with the working party where I had been invited to respond to a draft report in which the conclusion was that my academic freedom had not been breached, a conclusion I agreed with. What I did not agree with was that there was no recognition of the pressure to which I had been subjected while sustaining my academic freedom. In the clip I think you may feel a disturbing shock in the recognition of the power of my anger in the expression of energy and my passion for academic freedom and academic responsibility. Following my meeting with the working party, the report that went to Senate acknowledged that the reason my academic freedom had not been breached was because of my persistence in the face of pressure. This phrase, 'persistence in the face of pressure', is a phrase I continue to use in comprehending my meaning of Walton's standard of judgement of spiritual resilience gained through connection with a loving dynamic energy (Walton, 2008).

I have included this video clip on the grounds of authenticity. To understand the educational significance of the video of my keynote of March 2008, in my explanations of educational influence, requires an understanding of the significance of the rechannelling of the energy in the anger in the above video. I expressed this rechannelling in the keynote. This rechannelling was related to a persistence in the face of pressure. This persistence was possible through remaining open to the flows of loving dynamic energy in the passion for improving practice and contributing to educational knowledge (Whitehead, 2008, pp. 117–118).

In this presentation, my intention is to clarify and communicate my meanings of a living logic for educational research in the course of its emergence in my practice as an educational researcher in the knowledge-creating enquiry, 'How do I improve what I am doing?' The meanings are expressed both ostensively and lexically in the process of the evolution and growth of my educational knowledge in my educational research programme between 1970 and 2013. The growth of my educational knowledge includes the integration of ostensive expressions of meanings that are clarified through the experience of empathetic resonance with digitalised visual data, within a living logic.

One method I use to enhance the validity of my explanations of educational influence in learning is derived from Habermas' (1976, pp. 2–3) ideas about communication and the evolution of society:

> The speaker must choose a comprehensible expression (verständlich) so that speaker and hearer can understand one another. The speaker must have the intention of communicating a true (wahr) proposition (or a propositional content, the existential presuppositions of which are satisfied) so that the hearer can share the knowledge of the speaker. The speaker must want to express his intentions truthfully (wahrhaftig) so that the hearer can believe the utterance of the speaker (can trust him). Finally, the speaker must choose an utterance that is right (richtig) so that the hearer can accept the utterance and speaker and hearer can agree with one another in the utterance with respect to a recognized normative background. Moreover, communicative action can continue undisturbed only as long as participants suppose that the validity claims they reciprocally raise are justified (Habermas, 1976, pp. 2–3).

I have formed four questions that I ask a validation group to respond to, including any others that they wish to respond to:

1. How could I enhance the comprehensibility of my explanation?
2. How could I strengthen the evidence I use to justify the assertions I make?
3. How could I deepen and extend my understanding of the sociohistorical and sociocultural influences on my writings and my practice?
4. How could I enhance my authenticity in the sense of showing over time and interaction that I am truly committed to living as fully as I can the values that I claim to use to give meaning and purpose to my life of enquiry?

A characteristic of the growth of my educational knowledge is the continuing extension of deepening my cognitive range and concerns with propositional theories. This now includes the integration of the following insights from Biesta (2006), Derrida (1995, 1997) and Deleuze (2001).

My cognitive range now includes Beista's idea on moving from a language of learning to a language of education with a responsibility of the educator not only lying in the cultivation of "worldly spaces" in which the encounter with otherness and difference is a real possibility, but also extending to asking "difficult questions": questions that summon us to respond responsively and responsibly to otherness and difference in our own, unique ways (p. ix). I use Biesta's distinction between learning as acquisition and learning as responding and agree that learning as responding is educationally the more significant, as I believe that education not only is about the transmission of knowledge, skills and values, but also 'is concerned with the individuality, subjectivity, or personhood of the student, with their "coming into the world" as unique, singular beings.' (p. 27).

My cognitive range and concern are extending as I engage with Derrida's understandings of democracy, responsibility and the 'Gift of Death'. My commitment and understanding of democracy has rested in Dewey's work on *Democracy and Education* and the use of democracy as a procedural principle by Richard Peters (1966) in his *Ethics and Education*. Derrida challenges this idea by asking whether it is possible to keep the old name 'democracy' but to open out to the future, or rather, to the 'remaining to come' of a certain democracy:

> For democracy remains to come; this is its essence in so far as it remains: not only will it remain indefinitely perfectible, hence always insufficient and future, but, belonging to the time of the promise, it will always remain, in each of its future times, to come: even when there is democracy, it never exists, it is never present, it remains the theme of a non-presentable concept (Derrida, 1997, p. 306).

Derrida also asks: on what condition is responsibility possible? He answers that it is on the condition that the good is no longer a transcendental objective, a relation between objective things, but the relation to the other, a response to the other; an experience of personal goodness and a movement of intention. I find that this resonates with my movement of an intention that carries hope for the future of humanity. I accept Derrida's point that responsibility demands irreplaceable singularity and that it is only the apprehension of death that can give this irreplaceability:

> What gives me my singularity, namely, death and finitude, is what makes me unequal to the infinite goodness of the gift that is also the first appeal to responsibility. Guilt is inherent in responsibility because responsibility is always unequal to itself: one is never responsible enough. One is never responsible enough because one is finite but also because responsibility requires two contradictory movements. It requires one to respond as oneself and as irreplaceable singularity, to answer for what one does, says, gives; but it also requires that, being good and through goodness, one forget or efface the origin of what one gives (1995, p. 51).

My cognitive range and concern are also extending as I engage with Deleuze's (2001) understandings of 'defying judgement', 'immanence' and 'difference'. In recognising my commitment to bring new living standards of judgement into the Academy for legitimating contributions to educational knowledge I am challenged by Deleuze's criticism of philosophical judgement where he claims that philosophy degenerated as it developed through history, that it turned against itself and has been taken in by its own mask:

> Instead of linking an active life and an affirmative thinking, thought gives itself the task of judging life, opposing to it supposedly higher values, measuring it against these values, restricting and condemning it... Philosophy becomes nothing more than taking the census of all the reasons man gives himself to obey... All that remains then is an illusion of critique and a phantom of creation. For nothing is more opposed to the creator than the carrier. To create is to lighten, to unburden life, to invent new possibilities of life. The creator is legislator – dancer (pp. 68–69).

In Deleuze's philosophy, life does not function as a transcendent principle of judgement but as an immanent process of production or creation. Judgement operates with pre-existing criteria that can never apprehend the creation of the new, and what is of value can only come into existence by 'defying judgement' (Smith, 1998, p. iii).

I believe that my explanations of educational influence with their living logic retain an openness to the possibilities that life permits. Deleuze's point about defying judgement reminds me to be aware of the dangers of deluding myself and that I am killing off creativity by judging life in an illusion of critique and in the imposition of inappropriate standards of judgement. Hence my inclusion of 'living standards of judgement' that are clarified and communicated in the course of their emergence in practice, rather than being pre-existing criteria that are imposed in making a judgement.

I am also challenged by Deleuze's notion of immanence. The immanent event is actualised in a state of things and of the lived that makes it happen. I relate such a process of actualisation to the creation of a living-educational-theory that explains a present practice in terms of an evaluation of the past together with an intention to create something in the future which does not yet exist. It is the living that can make it happen. Because of the inclusion of my own irreplaceable singularity, my 'I' within my living-educational-theory I am still working to understand the significance for my research of Deleuze's idea of 'a plane of immanence':

The plan of immanence is itself actualized in an object and a subject to which it attributes itself. But however inseparable an object and a subject may be from their actualization, the plane of immanence is itself virtual, so long as the events that populate it are virtualities. Events or singularities give to the plane all their virtuality, just as the plane of immanence gives virtual events their fully reality. The event considered as non-actualized (indefinite) is lacking in nothing. It suffices to put it in relation to its concomitants: a transcendental field, a plane of immanence, a life, singularities (2001, p. 31).

As I continue to engage with developing a better understanding of the relationships between 'I' and 'We' and use the term i-we to represent a dynamic relationship between 'I' and 'We', I am exploring Rajchman's (2000) point in *The Deleuze Connections* where he focuses on what is capable of bringing us together without abolishing what makes us singular:

Multiplicity is not diversity, and making it requires another conception of Life – it is rather as if, under the "second nature" of our persons and identities, there lay a prior potential Life capable of bringing us together without abolishing what makes us singular. (Rajchman, 2000, p. 82).

In focusing on the nature of a dynamic of i-we relations which includes a pooling of energy within which we retain our unique and irreplaceable singularity, I am engaging with Deleuze's idea of Difference:

Opening is an essential feature of univocity. The nomadic distributions or crowned anarchies in the univocal stand opposed to the sedentary distributions of analogy. Only there does the cry resound: 'Everything is equal!' and 'Everything returns!' However, this 'Everything is equal' and this 'Everything returns 'can be said only at the point at which the extremity of difference is reached. A single and same voice for the whole thousand-voiced multitude, a single and same Ocean for all the drops, a single clamour of Being for all beings: on condition that each being, each drop and each voice has reached the state of excess – in other words, the difference which displaces and disguises them and, in turning upon its mobile cusp, causes them to return. (1994, p. 304).

Conclusion

A living logic for educational research has emerged from the enquiry, 'How do I improve what I am doing in my professional practice?' It has emerged in the logic that characterises the explanations, or living-theories, produced by practitioner-researchers as they explain their educational influences in their own learning, in the learning of others and in the learning of the social formations in which we live, work and research. The explanations include insights from both propositional and dialectical theories of education and constitute the growth of an individual's educational knowledge. The living logic includes both living contradictions and a relationally dynamic awareness of space and boundaries. The meanings of the living logic for educational research required both ostensive expressions of meaning communicated through digital visual data and lexical definitions of meaning. The living logic remains in a direct relationship with the practical, values-laden enquiry, 'How do I improve what I am doing?', and the explanations of educational influence in learning that are produced in such enquiries. The living logic distinguishes a form of rationality that can integrate insights from propositional and dialectical theories without denying the rationality of these logics. A living logic for educational research, with its requirement of visual data for the communication of meanings of the expression of embodied values as explanatory principles, has implications for extending the present solely text-based publications of BERA into multimedia, online journals.

References

Biesta, G.J.J. (2006) *Beyond Learning: Democratic Education for a Human Future*. Boulder: Paradigm Publishers.

Deleuze, G. (2001) *Pure Immanence: Essays on A Life*. New York: Zone Books.

Deleuze, G. (1994) *Difference and Repetition*. Translated by Paul Patton. London: Athlone Press.

Derrida, J. (1997) *The Politics of Friendship*. Translated by George Collins. London: Verso.

Derrida, J. (1995) *The Gift of Death*. Translated by David Wills. Chicago: University of Chicago Press.

Hirst, P. (Ed.) (1983) *Educational Theory and Its Foundation Disciplines*. London: Routledge and Kegan Paul.

Ilyenkov, E. (1977) *Dialectical Logic*. Moscow: Progress Publishers.

Popper, K. (1963) *Conjectures and Refutations*. Oxford: Oxford University Press.

Marcuse, H. (1964) *One Dimensional Man*. London: Routledge and Kegan Paul,

Rajchman, J. (2000) *The Deleuze Connections*. London: The MIT Press.

Smith, D.W. (1998) in Deleuze, G. (1998) *Essays Critical and Clinical*. Translated by Daniel W. Smith and Michael A. Greco. London: Verso.

Whitehead, J. (1972) *A preliminary investigation of the process through which adolescents acquire scientific understanding*. Unpublished MA dissertation, University of London.

Whitehead, J. (1999) *How Do I Improve My Practice? Creating A Discipline Of Education Through Educational Enquiry*. PhD thesis University of Bath. Retrieved 8 December 2017 from http://www.actionresearch.net/living/jackwhitehead2.shtml.

Whitehead, J. (2008) Using a living-theory methodology in improving practice and generating educational knowledge in living theories. *Educational Journal of Living Theories*, 1(1);

103–126. Retrieved 3 August 2013 from http://ejolts.net/node/80.

Whitty, G. (2005) Education(al) research and education policy making: is conflict inevitable? Presidential Address to the British Educational Research Association, University of Glamorgan, 17 September 2005. *British Educational Research Journal*, 32(2); 159–176.

PAPER SEVEN.

Whitehead, J. (2014) Enacting Educational Reflexivity in Supervising Research into Creating Living-Educational-Theories. *Journal of Educational Research for Social Change* 3(2); 81–93.

This paper focuses on the importance of educational reflexivity, not only in supervising research into the creation of living-educational-theories, but also in generating valid explanations of educational influences in supervising the creation of these theories.

At the heart of these explanations are educational and social relationships that are relationally dynamic and that connect with educational influences in the learning of social formations. This awareness of such relationships are at the heart of educational reflexivity in supervising the creation of living-educational-theories.

The distinction between reflection and reflexivity is an important one in explaining educational influences in learning. By reflection I am meaning an explicit awareness of what one is doing, thinking and feeling. By reflexivity I am meaning an explicit awareness of the principles that are guiding one's doing, thinking and feeling. These principles include a relational dynamic awareness of space and boundaries.

PAPER SEVEN.

Enacting Educational Reflexivity in Supervising Research into Creating Living-Educational-Theories

Abstract

To show how enacting reflexivity in research supervision in creating a living-educational-theory can address the notion of self in ways that go beyond navel-gazing in both improving practice and generating knowledge in making scholarly, academically legitimate, and original contributions to educational knowledge. This paper on educational reflexivity in supervision stresses the importance of clarifying and communicating the values that carry hope for the flourishing of humanity in explanations of educational influence from self-study researchers. In the same way that not all learning is educational, not all reflexivity supports the values that carry hope for the flourishing of humanity. Hence, the paper is focused on educational reflexivity in supervision to emphasise the importance of living these values as fully as possible in the creation of living-educational-theories.

Keywords: educational reflexivity; supervising research; living-educational-theories.

Introduction

This contribution responds to the aims of the special issue by foregrounding the relational dimensions of enacting reflexivity through critical perspectives in educational research into research supervision. It includes an engagement with self-study research, across academic disciplines and institutional contexts in South Africa and internationally, in grappling with complex quest ions such as, "How does reflexivity influence my research supervision?" It includes a Living Theory approach to educational research that contributes to both a representation of the social world, and to influencing the social world in a way that enhances the flow of values that contribute to the flourishing of humanity with Ubuntu (Charles, 2007). An English translation is "I am because we are". More details of Ubuntu are given below.

A living-educational-theory is an explanation produced by a self-study researcher to explain the educational influence in his or her own learning, in the learning of others, and in the learning of the social formations in which we live, work and research (Whitehead, 2008, 2012a). The self studied is the ontological, relational self whose explanations and standards of judgement are constituted by that self's life-affirming and life-enhancing values. These are clarified and communicated as they emerge through the research.

Living Theory research is distinguished from a living-educational-theory in terms of the abstract, general principles that can be used to characterise this approach to research. In contrast to these general principles, a living-educational-theory is the unique explanation produced by an individual. I shorten living-educational-theory to living-theory in this paper.

A distinction is also drawn between reflection and reflexivity. By reflection I mean a process of consciously thinking about our experiences, feelings, actions and responses through which we learn in self-study-enquiries of the kind, "How do I improve what I am doing?" By reflexivity I mean a process through which we clarify and communicate the ontological values we use to give our lives meaning and purpose, and which form the explanatory principles and living standards of judgement in our explanations of educational influence in self-study enquiries of the "How do I improve what I am doing?" kind.

Approach

The approach generated through enacting educational reflexivity into research supervision is known as Living Theory research (Whitehead, 2008, 2012b). This is grounded in what Dadds and Hart (2001, p. 169) referred to as methodological inventiveness. In this approach, self-study researchers explore the implications of asking, researching and answering questions of the kind, "How do I improve what I am doing?" The "I" is a relational "I" perhaps best represented as i~we to recognise the mutual influence of an individual with other/s in relational contexts. Insights into an Ubuntu way of being (Mandela, 2006) are drawn on, to distinguish the values that carry hope for the flourishing of humanity. My living-theory methodology draws insights from approaches such as Action Research and others such as those Cresswell (2007) summarised: Phenomenology, Case Study, Narrative Research, Ethnography, and Grounded Theory. The approach has much in common with Autoethnography (Ellis, Adams and Bochner, 2011, p. 273) in that the researcher seeks to describe and systematically analyse personal experience in order to understand cultural experience. It differs with its emphasis on the priority given to the knowledge-creating capacities of the individual. A living-theory methodology also engages in making contributions to the generation of a culture of enquiry (Delong, 2002, 2013, 2014) as well as understanding cultural experience and influence.

The approach also draws on digitalised visual data from professional practice in a process of empathetic resonance (Whitehead, 2012b). Huxtable (2009) described how this can be used to clarify and communicate the meanings of the embodied expressions of energy-flowing, ontological values that the self-study researcher uses to give meaning and purpose to existence and to explain educational influences in learning. This approach informs many living-theories, such as those in the December 2013 issue of the *Educational Journal of Living Theories*. That issue, with contributions from Delong (2013), Campbell (2013), Griffin (2013) and myself (Whitehead, 2013), is particularly relevant to this paper on research supervision because it explains how I influenced, as supervisor, Delong's living-theory doctorate and how Delong influenced, as supervisor, the living-theory master's dissertations of both Campbell and Griffin.

I am also using the values I identify as carrying hope for the flourishing of humanity, to distinguish what I mean by a critical perspective in my research supervision. By a critical perspective, I am not meaning the application of critical theory (Carr and Kemmis, 1986) to the generation of a living-educational-theory. This is because of a limitation in the application of any pre-existing theory as the dominating explanation in the generation of a living-educational-theory. In generating a living-educational-theory, an individual transcends the limitations of applying abstract concepts to explain his or her educational influence. An individual's living-educational-theory is unique and irreplaceable. It can draw insights from the conceptual frameworks of existing theories but always engages with these frameworks in a creative and critical way.

Being Critical and Enhancing Reflexivity

In enacting reflexivity in creating a living-educational-theory it is always possible to strengthen the objectivity of the explanation where objectivity is understood, in Popper's (1975, p. 45) terms, to be grounded in intersubjective criticism in the mutual rational controls of critical discussion. To overcome limitations in the subjective grounding of knowledge-claims, and criticisms of navel-gazing or being merely anecdotal, I use four questions with my students. These are derived from Habermas' (1976, pp. 2–3) four criteria of social validity in validation groups of between three and eight peers.

The questions are:
1) How can I enhance the comprehensibility of my explanation?
2) How can I strengthen the evidence I use to justify my assertions or claims to knowledge?
3) How can I deepen and extend my sociohistorical and sociocultural understandings of their influence in my writings and practice?

4) How can I improve the authenticity of my explanations in showing over time and interaction that I am truly committed to living as fully as possible the ontological values I claim to hold?

As well as stressing the importance of enhancing social validity in relation to the explanations produced by my students, I always stress the importance of their personal responsibility for telling the truth as they see it, in terms of Polanyi's (1958) post-critical philosophy. In this philosophy, an individual decides to understand the world from his or her point of view as a person claiming originality and exercising with universal intent. The democratic processes of enhancing criticism in a validation group, using the above questions, do not determine the truth of an explanation. The individual researchers accept responsibility for telling truth as they see it with the help of insights from a validation group.

The critical perspective I am using is focused on the use of the ontological values of the individual. These are the values individuals use to give meaning and purpose to their lives and to which they hold themselves accountable. These values are the explanatory principles they use to explain their educational influences in learning, and the critical principles they use in evaluating the validity of their claims to be improving their practice. This is not to deny the value of critical theory in unmasking the political, economic and cultural hegemonies that can distort our understandings of the sociohistorical and sociocultural influences in our writings and practice. It is, however, to insist that living-educational-theories transcend the limitations in critical theory to explain the educational influences of individuals in their own learning, in the learning of others, and in the learning of the social formations in which we live, work and research.

Results

The following brief overview of the results is focused on the aim of showing how enacting reflexivity in supervising living-educational-theories for higher degrees can address the notion of self in both improving practice and generating knowledge in making scholarly, academically legitimate, and original contributions to educational knowledge.

The evidence to justify this claim is focused on the living-educational-theory doctorates, including my own, that have been legitimated as original contributions to educational knowledge. I include the original contribution in my doctorate because of the principles I clarified and communicated in distinguishing my educational reflexivity. I also include this contribution because of the importance my students have given to seeing me research my own practice alongside their own research as I practise and evolve the living of the principles of reflexivity that I bring into my supervision.

All Living Theory researchers enact reflexivity in clarifying and communicating their meanings of the embodied expressions of the ontological values that form the explanatory principles in their explanations of influence. When I supervise Living Theory research my focus is on the life-enhancing values of the researcher, which form their explanatory principles, because they are the values that individuals use to give their lives meaning and purpose and to which they hold themselves accountable for living as fully as possible in their practice.

The evidence for these claims is publicly available from the online database at http://www.actionresearch.net/living/living.shtml. It includes more than 30 of the living-theory doctorates I supervised to successful completion between 1996 and 2012 that explicitly enact this reflexivity. The living-theory doctorates of Phillips (2011) and Charles (2007) could be of particular interest to researchers in South Africa because of the inclusion of Ubuntu ways of being as explanatory principles and living standards of judgement to which the researchers held themselves accountable.

I shall now focus on how I enact educational reflexivity in my supervision as I explain my educational influence in my own learning, in the learning of others, and in the learning of the social formations in which the research is located. These explanations are related. In explaining my educational influence in the learning of others, I recognise the validity of including insights from what I have learned of my educational influence in my own learning. For example, I stress the importance of the influence of social formations in the learning of myself and of others. This is because whatever we do is located in particular social contexts that influence what we do; hence the importance of including an understanding of the sociohistorical and sociocultural influences in explanations of educational influences in learning.

The relationship between these three explanations has been a continuously evolving characteristic of my enacting reflexivity in my supervision.

i) Enacting educational reflexivity in explaining my educational influence in my own learning

Here are three principles that distinguish the enactment of my educational reflexivity. I include these in explaining my educational influences in my own learning and that I bring into my supervision.

The first principle is recognising my "I" as a living contradiction through the use of visual data. By a living contradiction, I mean that one's "I" in exploring the implications of asking, researching, and answering a question of the kind, "How do I improve what I am doing?" holds together the experience of holding an ontological value, and of negating the value. It is important to recognise that the experience of existing as a living contradiction may be grounded in a social context where the contradiction is not from self but from others or from social formations.

The second principle is the decision of personal knowledge above, taken from Polanyi (1958). This principle is particularly important in enacting educational reflexivity by helping to resist the hegemonic pressures in academic cultures to explain one's own life and influences in terms of the abstractions of conceptual theories.

The third principle is the use of multimedia narratives for clarifying and communicating the meanings of embodied expressions of ontological values as explanatory principles in explanations of educational influences in learning.

a) Recognising "I" as a living contradiction.

I cannot overemphasise the importance of recognising oneself as a living contradiction in one's practice. In my case, I believed that I had established enquiry learning in my science classrooms when teaching science in a London comprehensive school during 1972–73. The inspectorate provided me with a video camera and recorder and asked that I explore its potential as an educational aid in the science department where I was Head of Science. I turned the video on myself and viewed myself teaching science. My shock in seeing myself as a living contradiction was in recognising that I believed that I had established enquiry learning in which pupils were asking their own questions and that I was responding to their questions. The video showed that I was providing the pupils with the questions and that not one of the pupils was asking their own question. This triggered my imagination to think of ways in which I could improve my practice, and within eight weeks I could show evidence that some of the pupils were asking their own questions and that I was responding to their questions. This quality of reflexivity in learning to question my own assumption has remained with me and I emphasise it in my research supervision.

b) Learning to resist the imposition of abstract conceptual theories on explanations of educational influence.

My second experience of enacting educational reflexivity was in the mixed ability exercise in science (Whitehead, 1976a, 1976b) when I researched, with six teachers over some 18 months, improving learning for 11–14-year-olds in mixed ability science groups. In conversation with the teachers, I asked about their concerns and what mattered to them. Martin Hyman, one of the teachers, explained:

> By the time they come to us a lot of people have lost their trust, confidence and eagerness to learn. We have to start trying to get it back and we succeed only

partially. All the children, even the non-exam children are bound by the constraints of teachers who feel obliged to cover exam syllabuses. I think this is where the confidence goes. (As cited in Whitehead, 1976b, p. 3).

Hyman highlighted the importance of trust, confidence and eagerness to learn as values that he held himself accountable to, and which distinguished his reflexivity.

My own learning in this research was focused on a mistake I made in my first research report (Whitehead, 1976a) in which I explained the learning of the teachers in terms of academic models of teaching and learning, evaluation, and innovation. My academic colleagues praised the report for the way I had used these academic models. After I submitted this report to the teachers, they all commented that they understood the way I had explained with the use of academic models, but that they could not see themselves in the explanation. Immediately this criticism was made, I could see that it was justified. I had replaced the explanatory principles used by the teachers with the abstract conceptualisations of academic models. With the help of Paul Hunt, a former postgraduate education student in his first year of teaching, we reconstructed the report (Whitehead, 1976b) in a way that the other teachers accepted as containing valid explanations of their practice and learning. The constraining power of academic cultures to influence the explanations of individuals within the theoretical frameworks of abstract theories continues (Whitehead, 2014a).

This second report also explicated, for the first time in my research, an action-reflection cycle for exploring the implications of asking, researching and answering questions of the kind, 'How do I improve what I am doing?' This action-reflection cycle was constituted by:

- expressing concerns when values are not being lived as fully as they could be;
- revealing the values that explain why the individual is concerned;
- developing and choosing an action plan to enact;
- acting and gathering data to make a judgement on educational influence;
- evaluating the educational influences in learning;
- producing an explanation of educational influences in learning and submitting this to a validation group.

This action-reflection cycle marks a transformation from reflection to reflexivity in explicating my explanatory principles. The action-reflection cycle was used to explain how the research was carried out. The action-reflection cycles were also useful in clarifying and communicating the meanings of the embodied energy-flowing values in the course of their emergence in practice. These values were used as explanatory principles in explaining the educational influences of individuals in their own learning and in the learning of others.

c) Using multimedia narratives with digital video for clarifying and communicating meanings of embodied expressions of ontological values.

I have analysed and explained the enacting of my educational reflexivity in the creation of my living-educational-theory, as an explanation of my educational influence in my own learning, in several publications (Whitehead, 1985, 1989, 1999, 2008, 2013). In the most recent (Whitehead, 2013) I focused on the use of a multimedia narrative to communicate the meaning of the expression of embodied values of loved into learning with Jacqueline Delong, Liz Campbell and Cathy Griffin:

We do not want to overload you with all the material in the following video, but we hope that you will access minutes 11:14 to 12:33 of Jackie, Liz and Jack in a conversation about our enquiry and presentation for the American Educational Research Association (AERA) 2013.

Video 1: Loved into Learning A
http://www.youtube.com/watch?v=5MPXeJMc0gU
During minutes 11:14 to 12:33, the conversation consists of:

Jack: Your phrase, loved into learning . . . you experienced this being loved into learning with Jackie and possibly some of the other participants on the master's programme.

[Liz is nodding and smiling.]

Jack (11:34): Could I just check that? It seemed very important because I don't think Jackie and myself have focused on Jackie's influence in those terms, yet it seemed really important to you that you had experienced that loved into learning that you were able then to communicate, I think, to your own students.

Liz (12:01): That's exactly the point I was trying to make, Jack, and I have written about it before in different pieces in my master's and in something I did in your class, Jackie.

Jackie: Yes.

Liz: I don't know if I actually called it loved into learning, but that is my concise way of explaining what happened.

I was introduced to the idea of being loved into learning in a conversation where Cathy and Liz explained Jackie's influence in their learning for their master's degree in terms of being loved into learning.

Video 2: Loved into Learning B

http://www.youtube.com/watch?v=qcDSqryJ6Jg

The image at 1:35 minutes of the 9:45-minute clip above is taken where we are talking about being loved into learning. As I move the cursor backwards and forwards around 1:35 minutes I experience the empathetic resonance (Huxtable, 2009) of Liz's, Cathy's, Jackie's, and my own energy-flowing value of being loved into learning. To communicate my embodied expression of meaning I need both the visual data showing the expressions above and my linguistic expression of being loved into learning. I am now bringing this meaning into my understanding of a culture of enquiry. Liz and Cathy also brought into Jackie's awareness the quality of loving into learning they experienced in Jackie's awareness the quality of loving into learning they experienced in Jackie's tutoring (Whitehead, 2013, 14–15).

ii) Enacting educational reflexivity in explaining my educational influence in supervising my students' research programmes.

In explaining my educational influence as a supervisor, I focus on my recognition and communication of the relational and ontological values the students use to give meaning and purpose to their life. By sharing my intuitions and insights about the students' expression of these values, their responses help me to evaluate their validity. The meanings of these values often take months to clarify and communicate in the course of their emergence in the practice of the enquiry. The importance of these meanings is that they often provide the explanatory principles and living standards of judgement that distinguish the student's original contribution to knowledge. Take, for example, Eden Charles' (2007) doctoral enquiry, *How can I bring Ubuntu as a living standard of judgement into the academy? Moving beyond decolonisation through societal re-identification and guiltless recognition.*

In the abstract below, I believe that there is clear evidence of the influence of my ideas in the language of 'a living-theory thesis', 'how I can improve my practice', 'a living standard of judgement' and 'visual narratives' are used to represent and help to communicate the inclusional meanings of these living standards of judgement'. In my dialogues with my students I enact my educational reflexivity by including these meanings, as principles, in all my supervisions. Students' integration of these ideas in their thesis in no way detracts from the uniqueness and originality of their own living-theory and contribution to knowledge. Part of the enactment of my educational reflexivity is in discerning the unique constellation of values and understandings that distinguish this originality and in sharing these understandings with my students.

The originality of Charles' thesis is in bringing Ubuntu, as a living standard of judgement, into the academy and in showing how the genesis of a living-theory can move beyond decolonisation through societal re-identification and guiltless recognition. These ideas may have particular significance to South African researchers because of the focus on Ubuntu:

Abstract

This is a living-theory thesis which traces my engagement in seeking answers to my question that focuses on how I can improve my practice as someone seeking to make a transformational contribution to the position of people of African origin. In the course of my enquiry I have recognised and embraced Ubuntu, as part of an African cosmology, both as my living practice and as a living standard of judgement for this thesis. It is through my Ubuntu way of being, enquiring and knowing that my original contribution to knowledge has emerged.

Two key approaches are identified and described in depth: 'guiltless recognition' and 'societal re-identification'. These emerge from a perception of self that is distinct within but not isolated in an awareness of 'inclusionality'. They are intimately related concepts. Guiltless recognition allows us to move beyond the guilt and blame that maintains separation and closes down possibility. It provides a basis for action and conception that moves us towards the imagined possibilities of societal re-identification with Ubuntu.

Both 'guiltless recognition' and 'societal re-identification' embody strategic and epistemological practices that move away from severing, colonising thought towards ways of being that open up new possibilities for people of African origin and for humanity generally.

Visual narratives are used to represent and help to communicate the inclusional meanings of these living standards of judgement. The narratives are focused on my work as a management consultant and include my work with Black managers. They explain my educational influence in creating and sustaining the Sankofa Learning Centre for Black young people in London. They include my living as a Black father seeking to remain present and of value to my son within a dominant discourse/ context in which this is a contradiction to the prevalent stereotype (Charles, 2007).

I think it worth stressing that as I supervise my students' research programmes I enact my educational reflexivity to explain my educational influence and I share ideas from my own research programme and those of other Living Theory researchers. I do this because I believe that this may be helpful to students in the generation of their own living-theories. I take care to explain to every student that there is a danger they should consider whether I am unwittingly imposing my ideas on them because of the differential power relations between student and supervisor. I am thinking here of the ideas that distinguish the principles in my educational reflexivity and that are worth emphasising:

- generating a living-educational-theory as an individual's explanation of their educational influence in their own learning, in the learning of others, and in the learning of the social formations that influence the practice and the writings;
- exploring the implications of asking, researching and answering questions of the kind, "How do I improve what I am doing?" in which "I" can exist as a living contradiction;
- using visual narratives with digital technology to clarify and communicate the meanings of embodied expressions of ontological and relational values in explanatory principles and living standards of judgement;
- submitting explanations of educational influence to a validation group of between three and eight peers with questions such as those described earlier.

The fact that so many (some 32, between 1996 and 2012) of my doctoral students have been recognised by internal and external examiners, as making their own original contributions to knowledge, is an indication that I have succeeded in enacting my educational reflexivity in a way that supported, rather than constrained, my students' creativity (Pound, Laidlaw and Huxtable, 2009).

iii) Enacting educational reflexivity in explaining educational influences in the learning of social formations.

Individuals cannot avoid the sociohistorical and sociocultural influences in their practice and their writings. Hence, it is important to demonstrate, in valid explanations of educational influence, that the individual is aware of these influences. This awareness is supported by the third question in a validation group: "How can I deepen and extend my understandings of the sociohistorical and sociocultural influences in my writing and practice?" In helping me to focus on this aspect of enacting educational reflexivity, I am indebted to the following insight offered by the late Susan Noffke about the process of generating living-educational-theory:

As vital as such a process of self-awareness is to identifying the contradictions between one's espoused theories and one's practices, perhaps because of its focus on individual learning, it only begins to address the social basis of personal belief systems. While such efforts can further a kind of collective agency (McNiff, 1988), it is a sense of agency built on ideas of society as a collection of autonomous individuals. As such, it seems incapable of addressing social issues in terms of the interconnections between personal identity and the claim of experiential knowledge, as well as power and privilege in society (Dolby, 1995; Noffke, 1991). The process of personal transformation through the examination of practice and self-reflection may be a necessary part of social change, especially in education; it is however, not sufficient. (Noffke, 1997, p. 329).

I agree with Noffke's criticism, which focuses on the need to address social issues in terms of power and privilege in society and the interconnections between personal identity and the claim of experiential knowledge.

In enacting educational reflexivity in the generation of living-educational-theories, it is not possible for every individual to address all of the social issues, economic, political, sociohistorical and sociocultural, that influence our enquiries. Many practitioner-researchers understandably focus on making changes in everyday workplace and community contexts without engaging with these wider social influences. Yet, as Susan Noffke has pointed out above, we will need to collectively engage in such issues if we are to contribute to both personal and social transformations in enhancing the flow of values that carry hope for the flourishing of humanity.

One complex value that all practitioner-researchers could hold themselves accountable to living as fully as possible is that of living global citizenship (Coombs, Potts and Whitehead, 2014). Each one of us is likely to give our own unique meaning to living global citizenship because of the particular constellation of values we use to give meaning and purpose to our lives. In fulfilling my own responsibility to this complex value, I bring it into my supervisions and public presentations on my research. For example, in a keynote presentation in Singapore on improving learning and practice in the workplace through Living Theory research (Whitehead, 2014b), I emphasised the importance of focusing on workplace learning in the creation of living-theories with values that carry hope for the flourishing of humanity. This inclusion of such values is of paramount importance in cultures such as Singapore and other economies, both successful and unsuccessful, where the language of economics dominates workplace learning. This is perhaps one of the world's greatest global challenges. To meet it will require supervisors of adult learnings in the workplace to support the generation of living-theories that are both focused on improving practice and contributing to economic well-being, and on enhancing the flow of values that carry hope for the flourishing of humanity.

When thinking of an example of living global citizenship, the life of Nelson Mandela is accepted by many as expressing this value – as I explained in my Mandela Day Lecture on 18 July 2011 (Whitehead, 2011). The idea of Mandela Day is that each one of us:

> … devote just 67 minutes of their time to changing the world for the better, in a small gesture of solidarity with humanity, and in a small step towards a continuous, global movement for good (http://www.unric.org/en/nelson-mandela-day/26957-can-you-spare-67-minutes-of-your-time-helping-others).

Mandela (2006), like Charles (2007) above, has stressed the importance of Ubuntu as a way of being and a value that carries hope for the flourishing of humanity.

In enacting educational reflexivity in explaining educational influences in the learning of social formations, I am stressing the importance of holding ourselves and each other to account for living, as fully as we can, Ubuntu ways of being in our social contexts.

Conclusion

Evidence has been provided to justify the claim that supervising the enacting of educational reflexivity in creating a living-educational-theory can both improve practice and generate knowledge in making scholarly, academically legitimate and original contributions to educational knowledge.

The implications of legitimating and spreading the influence of educational reflexivity in living-educational-theories are far-reaching as individuals explain their educational influence in their own learning, in the learning of others, and in the learning of social formations.

Perhaps the most significant implication is in contributing to a social movement, across cultural boundaries, that can contribute to enhancing the flow of ontological, energy-flowing values that carry hope for the flourishing of humanity in Ubuntu ways of being (Whitehead, 2011). This contribution will meet resistance from those pressures for economic globalisation that are contributing to increases in inequality around the world (Piketty, 2014; Stiglitz, 2013).

The supervision of living-educational-theories is not opposed to economic well-being. It includes economic well-being as an ontological value. The way this can be done has been demonstrated in Kaplan's (2013) research in South

Africa in generating her living-educational-theory with her question: "How do I use my living and lived experience to influence creative economic in dependence in others?"

Making these values the distinguishing qualities in enacting reflexivity in supervision is a necessary but not sufficient condition for making the world a better place to be. We must also make these values public in our explanations of how we are accounting to ourselves and to each other for living these values as fully as possible in supervising research into creating living-educational-theories.

References

Campbell, E. (2013) The heART of learning: Creating a loving culture-of-inquiry to enhance self-determined learning in a high school classroom. *Educational Journal of Living Theories*, 6(2), 45–6. Retrieved on 10 December 2016 from http://ejolts.net/node/211.

Carr, W. and Kemmis, S. (1986) *Becoming Critical*. London: Falmer Press.

Charles, E. (2007) How Can I Bring Ubuntu As A Living Standard Of Judgement Into The Academy? Moving Beyond Decolonisation Through Societal Re-Identification And Guiltless Recognition (PhD thesis, University of Bath, UK). Retrieved on 10 December 2016 from http://www.actionresearch.net/living/edenphd.shtml.

Coombs, S., Potts, M. and Whitehead, J. (2014) *International Educational Development and Learning through Sustainable Partnerships: Living Global Citizenship*. London: Palgrave Macmillan.

Cresswell, J.W. (2007) *Qualitative Inquiry & Research Design: Choosing Among Five Approaches*. California, USA: Sage.

Dadds, M. and Hart, S. (2001) *Doing Practitioner Research Differently*. London: RoutledgeFalmer.

Delong, J. (2002) How Can I Improve My Practice As A Superintendent Of Schools And Create My Own Living-Educational-Theory (PhD thesis, University of Bath, UK). Retrieved on 10 December 2016 from http://www.actionresearch.net/delong.shtml.

Delong, J. (2013) Transforming teaching and learning through living-theory action research in a culture-of-inquiry. *Educational Journal of Living Theories*, 6(2), 25–44. Retrieved on 10 December 2016 from http://ejolts.net/node/213.

Delong, J. (2014, May) How Has Living-Theory Research Transformed My Life And Influenced The World Around Me? Presentation at the Barn Sharing Session of the Bluewater District School Board Head Office, Canada. Retrieved on 10 December 2016 from http://www.spanglefish.com/ActionResearchCanada/index.asp?pageid=304629.

Ellis, C., Adams, T.E. and Bochner, A.P. (2011) Autoethnography: An Overview. *Historical Social Research*, 36(4); 273–290.

Feyerabend, P. (1975) *Against Method*. London: Verso.

Griffin, C. (2103) Transforming Teaching And Learning Practice By Inviting Students To Become Evaluators Of My Practice. *Educational Journal of Living Theories*, 6(2); 62–77. Retrieved on 10 December 2016 from http://ejolts.net/node/215.

Habermas, J. (1976) *Communication and the Evolution of Society*. London: Heinemann.

Huxtable, M. (2009) How Do We Contribute To An Educational Knowledge Base? A Response To Whitehead And A Challenge To BERJ. *Research Intelligence*, 107; 25–26.

Retrieved on 10 December 2016 from
http://www.actionresearch.net/writings/huxtable/mh2009beraRI107.pdf.

Kaplan, B. (2013) How Do I Use My Living And Lived Experience To Influence Creative Economic Independence In Others? (master's thesis, Durban University of Technology, South Africa. Retrieved on 10 December 2016 from http://www.actionresearch.net/living/kaplan/KaplanMTech032014.pdf.

Mandela, N. (2006) The Ubuntu Experience [video file]. Retrieved on 10 December 2016 from http://www.youtube.com/watch?v=ODQ4WiDsEBQ.

Noffke, S. (1997) Professional, Personal, And Political Dimensions Of Action Research. In M. Apple (Ed.), *Review of Research in Education*, Vol. 22. Washington, USA: AERA.

Phillips, I. (2011) My Emergent African Great Story 'Living I' As Naturally Including Neighbourhood, Embodying An Audacious Valuing Social Living Pedagogy And Imagining The Universe Luminously, As An Energetic Inclusion Of Darkness Throughout Light And Light In Darkness (PhD thesis, University of Bath, UK). Retrieved on 10 December 2016 from http://www.actionresearch.net/writings/phillips.shtml.

Piketty, T. (2014) *Capital in the Twenty-First Century*. London: Belknap.

Polanyi, M. (1958) *Personal Knowledge: Towards a Post-Critical Philosophy*. London: Routledge and Kegan Paul.

Popper, K. (1975) *The Logic of Scientific Discovery*. London: Hutchinson & Co.

Pound, R., Laidlaw, M. and Huxtable, M. (2009) *Jack Whitehead Validations*. Bath: Bear Flat Publishing. Retrieved on 10 December 2016 from http://www.actionresearch.net/writings/jack/jackvalidationsb.htm.

Stiglitz, J. (2013) *The Price of Inequality*. London: Penguin.

Whitehead, J. (1976a) An 11–14 Mixed Ability Project In Science: The Report On A Local Curriculum Development. Retrieved on 10 December 2016 from http://www.actionresearch.net/writings/jack/jwmaemarch1976all.pdf.

Whitehead, J. (1976b) *Improving Learning For 11- To 14-Year-Olds In Mixed Ability Science Groups*. Swindon: Wiltshire Curriculum Development Centre. Retrieved from http://www.actionresearch.net/writings/ilmagall.pdf.

Whitehead, J. (1985) An Analysis Of An Individual's Educational Development: The Basis For Personally Orientated Action Research. In M. Shipman (Ed.), *Educational Research: Principles, Policies & Practices* (pp. 97–108). London: Falmer. Retrieved on 10 December 2016 from http://www.actionresearch.net/writings/jack/jw1985analindiv.pdf.

Whitehead, J. (1989) Creating a living-educational-theory from questions of the kind, 'How do I improve my practice?' *Cambridge Journal of Education*, 19(1), 41–52. Retrieved on 10 December 2016 from http://www.actionresearch.net/writings/livtheory.html.

Whitehead, J. (1999) How Do I Improve My Practice? Creating A New Discipline Of Educational Enquiry (PhD thesis, University of Bath, UK). Retrieved on 10 December 2016 from http://www.actionresearch.net/living/jackwhitehead2.shtml.

Whitehead, J. (2008) Using A Living-Theory Methodology In Improving Practice And Generating Educational Knowledge In Living-Theories. *Educational Journal of Living Theories*, 1(1); 103–126. Retrieved on 10 December 2016 from http://www.actionresearch.net/writings/jack/jwLTM130608zhejiang.pdf.

Whitehead, J. (2011, July) Jack Whitehead's Mandela Day Lecture. Presented to Durban University of Technology, South Africa. Retrieved on 10 December 2016 from http://www.actionresearch.net/writings/jack/jwmandeladay2011.pdf.

Whitehead, J. (2012a) Educational Research For Social Change With Living-Educational-Theories. *Educational Research for Social Change*, 1(1), 5–21. Retrieved on 10 December 2016 from http://ersc.nmmu.ac.za/view_edition.php?v=1&n=1.

Whitehead, J. (2012b) *To Know Is Not Enough, Or Is It?* In To know is not enough: Action research as the core of educational research. Symposium conducted at the AERA Conference, Vancouver, Canada. Retrieved on 10 December 2016 from http://www.actionresearch.net/writings/jack/jwaera12noffke200212.pdf.

Whitehead, J. (2013) Evolving A Living-Educational-Theory Within The Living Boundaries Of Cultures-Of-Inquiry. *Educational Journal of Living Theories*, 6(2), 12–24. Retrieved on 10 December 2016 from http://ejolts.net/node/212.

Whitehead, J. (2014a, April) *How Does The Constraining Power Of Education Researchers Influence The Emergence Of Educational Knowledge And Theory?* Presentation at the Annual Conference of the American Educational Research Association, Philadelphia, USA. Retrieved on 10 December 2016 from http://www.actionresearch.net/writings/aera14/jwaera2014indiv110314.pdf.

Whitehead, J. (2014b, July) *Improving Learning And Practice In The Workplace Through Living-Theory Research*. Keynote presentation to a conference at the Institute for Adult Learning in Singapore. Retrieved on 10 December 2016 from http://www.actionresearch.net/writings/jack/jwsingapore2014paper.pdf.

Wolvaardt, E. (2013) Over The Conceptual Horizon Of Public Health: A Living-Theory Of Teaching Undergraduate Medical Students. (PhD thesis, University of Pretoria, South Africa). Retrieved on 10 December 2016 from http://www.actionresearch.net/writings/wolvaardtphd/Wolvaardtphd2013.pdf

PAPER EIGHT.

Justifying Your Creation of a Living-Theory Methodology in the Creation of Your Living-Educational-Theory: Notes for doctoral and master's students updated 28 January 2018.

Many practitioner-researchers who are registering for doctoral research in many different universities have explained to me that they feel under pressure from supervisors to choose their methodological approach at the beginning of their research journal. One of the distinguishing characteristics of Living Theory research is that the individual researcher generates their own living-theory methodology in the course of their enquiry and production of their own living-educational-theory. This trust that an appropriate methodology will emerge, rather than being chosen and applied, is grounded in the researchers' methodological inventiveness (Dadds and Hart, 2001).

In generating a living-theory methodology it is important to acknowledge the use of methods and insights from a range of methodological approach. These notes respond to Cresswell's ideas on: Narrative Research, Phenomenology, Grounded Theory, Ethnography and Case Studies; Ellis and Bochner's ideas on Auto-ethnography; Whitehead and McNiff's ideas on Action Research; Whitehead's ideas on Living Theory research and Tight's ideas on Phenomenography.

PAPER EIGHT.

Justifying Your Creation of a Living-Theory Methodology in the Creation of Your Living-Educational-Theory.

Responding to Cresswell's ideas on: Narrative Research, Phenomenology, Grounded Theory, Ethnography and Case Study; Ellis and Bochner's ideas on Autoethnography; Whitehead and McNiff's ideas on Action Research and Living Theory research; Tight's ideas on Phenomenography.

Notes for doctoral and master's students updated 28 January 2018

I am aware of the responses of some supervisors of master's dissertations and doctoral theses when they are presented with draft writings on an individual's living-educational-theory. They say that they want a fuller justification of the methodological approach used in relation to Narrative Research, Phenomenological Research, Grounded Theory research, Ethnographic Research or Case Study research. In my experience this kind of justification is not often useful to the student but is very helpful in revealing the methodological and epistemological assumptions in the supervisor's thinking.

I know that there can be some confusion about the different meanings of a method and methodology and I try to be clear about the following distinction. A method is a way of collecting data, or a technique of analysis. A methodology provides the rationale for how the research was carried out in generating theory. A methodology provides the theoretical analysis of the methods and principles associated with contribution to knowledge being made in the research. A methodology does not set out to provide solutions. It is worth repeating that a methodology is not the same as a method. A methodology offers the theoretical underpinning for understanding how the research was carried out.

I have found Cresswell's (2007, pp. 53–58) descriptions of five qualitative research approaches to Narrative Research, Phenomenology, Grounded Theory, Ethnography and Case Study to be one of the best introductory texts on these methodologies. For each of the five approaches Cresswell poses a definition, briefly traces the history of each approach, explores types of studies, introduces procedures involved in conducting a study, and indicates potential challenges in using each approach. He also reviews some of the similarities and differences among the five approaches 'so that qualitative researchers can decide which approach is best to use for their particular study'. I shall emphasise the point below that a researcher need not choose one of these methodologies. As a researcher your can draw insights from any of these approaches together with insights from Action Research,

Autoethnography and Phenomenography without choosing between them in the development of their own living-theory methodology as you create your living-educational-theory. You can access a 2008 paper of mine on using a living-theory methodology in improving practice and generating educational knowledge in living theories in the *Educational Journal of Living Theories (EJOLTS)* at http://ejolts.net/node/80.

Living Theory Research And A Living-Theory Methodology

A distinguishing feature of Living Theory research is that the researcher creates and publicly shares an explanation of their educational influence in their own learning, in the learning of others and in the learning of the social formations that influence the practice and understandings in enquiries of the kind, 'How do I improve what I am doing?' A Living Theory researcher recognises that there is no existing methodology that is appropriate for exploring the implications of asking, researching and answering the question, 'How do I improve what I am doing?' The reason that no existing methodology can answer the question is because of the dynamic nature of the question. 'What I am doing' is continuously changing with the evolution of both 'I' and context. Hence the necessity for the Living Theory researcher of recognising the need to create an appropriate living-theory methodology in the course of its emergence in researching and answering the question and in generating a unique living-theory. Whilst having to create their own living-theory methodology Living Theory researchers are fortunate in having access to a wide range of insights from other methodological approaches.

Here are the descriptions of the five approaches, distinguished by Cresswell (2007), followed by descriptions of Action Research, Autoethnography and Phenomenography that you might draw on in explaining why you need to go beyond the individual methodologies, or a combination of methodologies, in creating your own methodology as you generate your explanations of educational influences in learning in enquiries of the kind, 'How do I improve what I am doing?'

Dadds and Hart (2001) put the need for methodological inventiveness very clearly and this is the inventiveness that is needed to go beyond the following five approaches while drawing insights from the approaches where appropriate:

The importance of methodological inventiveness.

Perhaps the most important new insight for both of us has been awareness that, for some practitioner-researchers, creating their own unique way through their research may be as important as their self-chosen research focus. We had understood for many years that substantive choice was fundamental to the motivation and effectiveness of practitioner research (Dadds, 1995); that what practitioners chose to research was important to their sense of engagement and purpose. But we had understood far less well that how practitioners chose to research, and their sense of control over this, could be equally important to their motivation, their sense of identity within the research and their research outcomes (Dadds and Hart, p. 166, 2001).

If our aim is to create conditions that facilitate methodological inventiveness, we need to ensure as far as possible that our pedagogical approaches match the message that we seek to communicate. More important than adhering to any specific methodological approach, be it that of traditional social science or traditional action research, may be the willingness and courage of practitioners – and those who support them – to create enquiry approaches that enable new, valid understandings to develop; understandings that empower practitioners to improve their work for the beneficiaries in their care. Practitioner research methodologies are with us to serve professional practices. So what genuinely matters is the purposes of practice which the research seeks to serve, and the integrity with which the practitioner-researcher makes methodological choices about ways of achieving those purposes. No methodology is, or should be, cast in stone, if we accept that professional intention should be informing research processes, not pre-set ideas about methods of techniques... (Dadds and Hart, p. 169, 2001).

1) Cresswell Describes Narrative Research As Follows:

Narrative Research

Narrative research has many forms, uses a variety of analytic practices, and is rooted in different social and humanities disciplines (Daiute and Lightfoot, 2004). 'Narrative' might be the term assigned to any text of discourse, or, it might be text used within the context of a mode of enquiry in qualitative research (Chase, 2005), with a specific focus on the stories told by individuals (Polkinghorne, 1995). As Pinnegar and Daynes (2006) suggest, narrative can be both a method and the phenomenon of study. As a method, it begins with the experiences as lived and told stories of individuals. Writers have provided ways for analyzing and understanding the stories lived and told. I will define it here as a specific type of qualitative design in which 'narrative is understood as a spoken or written text giving an account of an event/action or series of events/actions, chronologically connected' (Czarniawska, 2004, p. 17). The procedures for implementing this research consist of focusing on studying one or two individuals, gathering data through the collection of their stories, reporting individual experiences and chronologically ordering (or using life course stages) the meaning of these experiences (pp. 53–54).

Cresswell describes a biographical study as a form of narrative study in which the researcher writes and records the experiences of another person's life. He says that:

Autobiography is written and recorded by the individuals who are the subject of the study (Ellis, 2004). A life history portrays an individual's entire life, while a personal experience story is a narrative study of an individual's personal experience found in single of multi episodes, private situations, or communal folklore (Denzin, 1989a) (p. 55).

A living-theory, as an explanation by an individual of their educational influences in their own learning and in the learning of others, can be understood as a form of narrative research in that it begins with the experiences as lived and told by the researcher. Within the narrative what distinguishes the story as a living-theory is that it is an explanation of the educational influences of the individual in their own learning and in the learning of others. Not all narratives are living-theories, but all living-theories are narratives.

2) Cresswell Describes Phenomenological Research As Follows:

Phenomenological Research

Whereas a narrative study reports the life of a single individual, a phenomenological study describes the meaning for several individuals of their lived experiences of a concept of a phenomenon. Phenomenologists focus on describing what all participants have in common as they experience a phenomenon (e.g. grief is universally experienced). The basic purpose of phenomenology is to reduce individual experiences within a phenomenon to a description of the universal essence (a 'grasp of the very nature of the thing'; van Manen, 1990, p. 177). To this end, qualitative researchers identify a phenomenon (an 'object' of human experience; van Manen, 1990, p. 163). This human experience may be a phenomenon such as insomnia, being left out, anger, grief, or undergoing coronary artery bypass surgery (Moustakas, 1994). The enquirer then collects data from persons who have experienced the phenomenon, and develops a composite description of the essence of the experience for all individuals. This description consists of 'what' they experienced and 'how' they experienced it. (Moustakas, 1994, pp. 57–58).

Living-theories are phenomenological in that they begin from the experience of the phenomenon the researcher is seeking to understand. The purpose of a living theory differs from the basic purpose of phenomenology in that the purpose of phenomenology is to produce a description of a universal essence, whilst the purpose of a living theory is to produce a unique explanation of the individual's educational influences in learning.

3) Cresswell Describes Grounded Theory Research As Follows:

Grounded Theory Research

Although a phenomenology emphasizes the meaning of an experience for a number of individuals, the intent of grounded theory study is to move beyond description and to generate or discover a theory, an abstract analytical scheme of a process (or action or interaction, Strauss and Corbin, 1998). Participants in the study would all have experienced the process, and the development of the theory might help explain practice or provide a framework for further research. A key idea is that this theory-development does not come 'off the shelf,' but rather is generated or 'grounded' in data from participants who have experienced the process (Strauss and Corbin, 1998). Thus, grounded theory is a qualitative research design in which the inquiry generates a general explanation (a theory) of a process, action, or interaction shaped by the views of a large number of participants. (Strauss and Corbin, 1998, pp. 62–63).

A living-theory is similar to a grounded theory in that the intent of a living-theory is to move beyond description and to generate a valid explanation for an individual's educational influence in his or her own learning and in the learning of others. Living Theory differs from Grounded Theory in that the theory is not an abstract analytic scheme of a process. A living-theory is an explanation for an individual's educational influence in learning where the explanatory principles are not abstract generalisations. The explanatory principles are the energy-flowing values and understandings the individual uses to give meaning and purpose to their life and to explain their educational influences in learning.

4) Cresswell Describes Ethnographic Research As Follows:

Ethnographic Research

Although a grounded theory researcher develops a theory from examining many individuals who share in the same process, action, or interaction, the study participants are not likely to be located in the same place or interacting on so frequent a basis that they develop shared patterns of behaviour/behaviours, beliefs, and language. An ethnographer is interested in examining these shared patterns, and the unit of analysis is larger than the 20 or so individuals involved in a grounded theory study. An ethnography focuses on an entire cultural group. Granted, sometimes this cultural group may be small (a few teachers, a few social workers), but typically it is large, involving many people who interact over time (teachers in an entire school, a community social work group). Ethnography is a qualitative design in which the researcher describes and interprets the shared and learned patterns of values, behaviour/behaviours, beliefs and language of a culture-sharing group (Harris, 1968). As both a process and an outcome of research (Agar, 1980), ethnography is a way of studying a culture-sharing group as well as the final, written product of that research. As a process, ethnography involves extended observations of the group, most often through participant observation, in which the researcher is immersed in the day-to-day lives of the people and observes and interviews the group participants. Ethnographers study the meaning of the behaviour, the language, and the interaction among members of the culture-sharing group (pp. 68–69).

A living-theory is similar to Ethnographic Research in paying attention to the cultural norms within which the researcher is acting and researching. It differs from Ethnographic Research in that it does not focus on an entire culture group. A living theory is an explanation of an individual's educational influence in their own learning, in the learning of others and in the social formations in which the researcher is living and working. In engaging with the cultural influences in the individual's learning, especially in the learning of social formations, living theorists include an understanding of cultural influences in the explanations of their educational influences in learning. These influences can be emphasised in the application of Habermas' (1976) four criteria of social validity, especially with the criterion of demonstrating an awareness of the normative background from within which the researcher is speaking and writing.

5) Cresswell Describes Case Study Research As Follows:

Case Study Research

The entire culture-sharing group in ethnography may be considered a case, but the intent in ethnography is to determine how the culture works rather than to understand an issue or problem using the case as a specific illustration. Thus, case study research involves the study of an issue explored through one or more cases within a bounded system (i.e., a setting, a context). Although Stake (2005) states that case study research is not a methodology but a choice of what is to be studied (i.e., a case within a bounded system), others present is as a strategy of inquiry, a methodology, or a comprehensive research strategy (Denzin and Lincoln, 2005; Marriam, 1998; Yin, 2003). I choose to view it as a methodology, a type of design in qualitative research, or an object of study, as well as a product of the inquiry. Case study research is a qualitative approach in which the investigator explores a bounded system (a case) or multiple bounded systems (cases) over time, through detailed, in-depth data collection involving multiple sources of information (e.g., observations, interviews, audiovisual material, and documents and reports), and reports a case description and case-based themes. For example, several programs (a multi-site study) or a single program (a within-site study) may be selected for study (p. 73).

A living-theory may sometimes be mistaken as a Case Study. Stake (2005) refers to Case Study as a choice of what is to be studied within a bounded system. Living-theories generated from a perspective of inclusionality, as a relationally dynamic awareness of space and boundaries, are aware of the experience and expression of a life-affirming and unbounded energy flowing through the cosmos. The main difference between a Case Study and a living-theory is that a Case Study is a study of a bounded system whilst the explanatory principles of living-theories are not constrained by a bounded system. Living-theories articulate explanatory principles in terms of flows of life-affirming energy, values and understandings that are transformatory and not contained within a bounded system.

If you are conducting an enquiry of the kind 'How do I improve what I am doing?' with the intention of improving your practice and generating knowledge in your living-educational-theory, I think that you will need to embrace Dadds and Hart's (2001) idea of methodological inventiveness in the creation of both your living-educational-theory and your living-theory methodology (Whitehead, 2009).

6) Action Research

In 1953 Stephen Corey produced the first textbook on Action Research in education on 'Action Research to Improve School Practices'. On 8 January 2016 a search on Google on Action Research generated over 16,000,000 references. There are now many different schools of Action Research. Most include some form of action-reflection cycles of planning, acting, evaluating and modifying. This method of enquiry, using an action planner, involves the Action Researcher studying their own practice in order to improve it.

An important text in the history of action research is Wilf Carr and Stephen Kemmis' (1983) *Becoming Critical: Knowing Through Action Research*, with many of these ideas included in their 1986 publication on *Becoming Critical: Education, Knowledge and Action Research*. Carr and Kemmis applied Habermas' critical theory to distinguish their critical approach to action research from other approaches. They retained the action-reflection cycles in their action planner whilst emphasising the priority of sociopolitical, historical and cultural influences in the knowledge generated through action research.

In several other publications Jean McNiff and myself (McNiff and Whitehead, 2009a and b, 2011) stressed the importance of the knowledge created by action researchers as they researched the processes of improving their practice, without giving a priority to explanatory principles derived from social science theories and methods.

McNiff and I also stressed the importance of individuals generated their living-educational-theories in their action research in our 2006 publication, *Action Research Living Theory*(Whitehead and McNiff, 2006).

7) Autoethnography

For me, the clearest response to the question, 'What is Autoethnography?', has been provided by Ellis and Bochner (2000):

> Autoethnography is an autobiographical genre of writing and research that displays multiple layers of consciousness, connecting the personal to the cultural. Back and forth autoethnographers gaze, first through an ethnographic wide-angle lens, focused outward on social and cultural aspects of their personal experience; then, they look inward, exposing a vulnerable self that is moved by and may move through, refract, and resist cultural interpretations (see Deck, 1990; Newmann, 1996; Reed-Danahay, 1997). As they zoom backwards and forward, inward and outward, distinctions between the personal and cultural become blurred, sometimes beyond distinct recognition. Usually written in first-person voice, autoethnographic texts appear in a variety of forms – short stories, poetry, fiction, novels, photographic essays, personal essays, journals, fragmented and layered writing, and social science prose. In these texts concrete action, dialogue, emotion, embodiment, spirituality, and self-consciousness are featured, appearing as relational and institutional stories affected by history, social structure, and culture, which themselves are dialectically revealed through action, feeling, thought, and language (p. 739).

As a Living Theory researcher I identify more closely with Autoethnography than the other methodologies whilst continuing to draw insights from the other methodologies. I particularly like the following about autoethnographic texts:

In these texts concrete action, dialogue, emotion, embodiment, spirituality, and self-consciousness are featured, appearing as relational and institutional stories affected by history, social structure, and culture, which themselves are dialectically revealed through action, feeling, thought, and language (p. 739).

My doctorate (Whitehead, 1999) can be seen, in the above sense, as an autoethnographic text. It is also a Living Theory autoethnography in the sense that the relational and institutional stories are presented within an explanation of my educational influence in my own learning, in the learning of others and in the learning of the social formations that influence my practice and understandings.

8) Phenomenography

Tight (2016) claims that the application of Phenomenography is arguably the only research design (so far) to have been developed substantially within higher education research by higher education researchers. Tight identifies Phenomenography as a research design and says that there is a need to differentiate research design from methodology and theory, as these three terms tend to be used in somewhat overlapping ways. Tight uses the term research design to refer to the overarching approach taken towards a particular research project. As such, Tight says that a research design typically encompasses distinctive methodological and theoretical positions or viewpoints (even if these are not recognised and articulated).

> Phenomenographers adopt a particular (albeit with some variations) methodological strategy for data collection and analysis. This typically involves the use of interviews as a method for collecting data on the phenomenon of current interest; though other forms of data, such as written responses, may also be used. All of the data collected is then treated collectively for the purposes of analysis, such that the focus is on the variations in understanding across the whole sample, rather than on the characteristics of individuals' responses (p. 320).

A Living Theory researcher might draw on such variations in understanding across a 'sample', in the generation of a living-theory, but the individual's explanation of educational influence in learning cannot be subsumed within an analysis from a phenomenographic analysis of a 'sample'.

References
Carr, W. and Kemmis S. (1983) *Becoming Critical: Knowing Through Action Research.* Melbourne: Deakin University Press.

Carr, W. and Kemmis, S. (1986) *Becoming Critical: Education, Knowledge and Action Research*. London: RoutledgeFalmer.

Corey, S. (1953) *Action Research to Improve School Practices*. New York: Teachers College, Columbia University.

Cresswell, J.W. (2007) *Qualitative Inquiry & Research Design: Choosing Among Five Approaches*. California, London, New Delhi: Sage.

Dadds, M. and Hart, S. (2001) *Doing Practitioner Research Differently*. London: RoutledgeFalmer.

Ellis, C. and Bochner, A.P. (2000) Autoethnography, Personal Narrative, Reflexivity: Researcher as subject, pp. 733–768 in Denzin, N. and Lincoln, Y. (2000) *Handbook of Qualitative Research*, second edition. Thousand Oaks, California: SAGE Publications.

McNiff, J. and Whitehead, J. (2011) *All you need to know about action research*. London: SAGE Publications.

McNiff, J. and Whitehead, J. (2009a) *You and Your Action Research Project*, third edition. London: Routledge.

McNiff, J. and Whitehead, J. (2009b) *Doing and Writing Action Research*. London: Sage.

Tight, M. (2016) Phenomenography: the development and application of an innovative research design in higher education research. *International Journal of Social Research Methodology*, 19(3); 319–338.

Whitehead, J. (1999) *How Do I Improve My Practice? Creating A Discipline Of Education Through Educational Enquiry*. PhD thesis, University of Bath. Retrieved 9 January 2016 from http://www.actionresearch.net/living/jackwhitehead2.shtml.

Whitehead, J. (2009) How do I influence the Generation of Living Educational Theories for Personal and Social Accountability in Improving Practice? Using a Living Theory Methodology in Improving Educational Practice, pp. 173–194, in Tidwell, D.L., Heston, M.L. and Fitzgerald, L.M. (Eds.) (2009) *Research Methods for the Self-Study of Practice*. Chicago: Springer.

Whitehead, J. and McNiff, J. (2006) *Action Research Living Theory*. London: Sage.

POSTSCRIPT MARCH 2018

Many people have visited my website over the years and told me they find the resources there very helpful but initially overwhelming and it was difficult to know where to start. So, I selected the papers from my website http://www.actionresearch.net for those looking for work that would help those who want to learn more about Living Theory research by doing it and developing their own living-educational-theories as a contribution to the flourishing of humanity. The papers I have chosen are arranged chronologically so you can see some of my learning journey in good company and the evolution of my understanding of Living Theory research.

I do hope that my willingness to share my journey will act as a stimulus for you to share your own. Such sharing could help to overcome a criticism that is often made of a living-educational-theory in relation to a traditional understanding of 'generalisability' in the sense of something applying to all. The number of living-educational-theorists is growing into a co-operative alliance in a social movement. This is contributing to a global influence on enhancing educational practices and extending and deepening the educational knowledge base of education with individual and community values that carry hope for the mass flourishing of humanity, including our own. I'm hoping that you will accept this invitation to share your own educational learning journey and to strengthen the co-operative alliances within our communities.

My next book will focus on the use of social media and digital visual data from Living Theory communities that are enhancing the influence of a social movement with values that carry hope for the mass flourishing of humanity.

References

Tetteh, E. (2017) *Keynotes for the 2018 ALARA World Congress.* Retrieved 31 January 2018 from http://www.actionresearch.net/writings/alara2018/alara2018keynotes.pdf

Whitehead, J. (2017) *Report on the CARN study day/Pre-Conference workshop for the 1st Global Assembly for Knowledge Democracy. Towards an ecology of knowledges* Retrieved 31 January 2018 from https://knowledgedemocracy.org/2017/02/15/report-on-the-carn-study-daypre-conference-workshop/.

Whitehead, J. (2018) *Learning how to contribute to a co-operative economy*: Notes for a meeting of the Bath Co-operative Alliance on 25 January 2018 at the Oriel Hall, Larkhall, Bath. Retrieved 31 January 2018 from http://www.actionresearch.net/writings/jack/jwcoopeconomy250118.pdf.

Whitehead, J., Delong, J. and Huxtable, M. (2018) *Where do we go from here in contributing to 'The Action Learning and Action Research Legacy for Transforming Social Change'?* Retrieved 31 January 2018 from http://www.actionresearch.net/writings/jack/jjdjwmhalara240118workprop.pdf.

INDEX

Plato 11, 13
Poland 90
Polanyi, Michael 15, 31, 36, 76, 101,
    104, 144, 146
Polkinghorne, D E 161
Popper, Karl 4, 7, 13, 23, 79, 109, 110,
    111, 127, 143
Potts, M 152
Pound, Robyn 50, 112, 113
Pritchard, M 20
Pylkkänen, P 28
Rajchman, J 136
Raybould, Jane 42
Rayner, Alan 75, 83, 97, 103, 107,
    110, 116, 130
Reed-Danahay, D 166
relational values 2, 45, 97, 151
Renowden, Jane 100, 102, 108
Research Intelligence 87, 107, 112
Riding, Karen 105, 121
Riding, Simon 105, 121
Roche, Mary 90, 91, 105
Rochon, R 99, 101
Rudduck, J 41
Ryle, G 75
Said, Edward 103
Sankofa Learning Centre 150
Sardello, R 108
Scholes-Rhodes, J 86
Schön, Donald 10, 65, 115
Schütz, Alfred 77, 78
Selmes, Cyril 42
Singapore 152
Smith, D W 135
Smith, P G 12
Snow, C E 47, 115
Socrates 13
South Africa 88, 90, 102, 107, 116,
    141, 145, 150
Spiro, Jane 87, 89, 90, 91, 121
St. Mary's College,
    Twickenham, UK 100, 102
Stake, R E 165
Stiglitz, J 153
Strauss, A 163
Sullivan, Bernie 90, 105, 105

Tasker, Mary 42
Tight, M 6, 157, 159, 167
Tillich, Paul 84
Tostberg, R E 12
Ubuntu 84, 107, 108, 111, 121, 141, 142,
    145, 149, 150, 153
University of Bath 5, 23, 24, 26, 27, 30,
    33, 34, 38, 45, 48, 50, 56, 58, 72, 74,
    77, 85, 90, 100, 101, 104, 105, 108,
    112, 121, 128
University of Glamorgan 105
University of Limerick 90, 97, 104, 105
University of London 100, 127
University of Manchester 97
University of Newcastle 121
University of Sussex 125
University of the Free State 107
University of the West of England
    113, 121, 123
USA 88, 102
Valéry, Paul 103
van Manen, M 162
Vasilyuk, F 116
Walker, R 18
Walton, Joan 84, 85, 87, 121, 132
Watkins, Peter 41, 42
Way To Professionalism In Education, A 71
Weber, S 56, 57
Wells, A S 63
Whitehead, Joan 42
Whitty, G 20, 41, 57, 62, 129
Wikman, Georg 28
Winter, R 36, 115, 116
Wittgenstein, Ludwig 13
Wood, L A 90
World Congress on Action Learning, Action
    Research and Process Management 23
Yin, R K 165
York St John University 100
Zeichner, K 48